HEALTH Mind SOUL

8 Steps To Finding Your Inner Peace

JEFF SIMPSON

Health Mind Soul

Living Your Optimal Life

Health Mind Soul
Copyright © 2020 by Jeff Simpson, Tara Clements

Tellwell Talent
www.tellwell.ca

ISBN
978-0-2288-3086-3 (Paperback)
978-0-2288-3087-0 (eBook)

I dedicate this book to my beautiful wife and daughter who have inspired me to be a better husband and father.

No matter what outcome awaits, I will always be grateful for the opportunity to inspire, teach and learn from others.

CONTENTS

INTRODUCTION

We must know where we've been if we want to know where we're going

~ JS

My name is Jeff Simpson. I'm a father, husband, fitness fanatic, spiritual being, and someone who genuinely loves life. I've been driven to be a better version of my old self. I genuinely want this book to inspire, help, educate, and remind us all that through those dark times, there's always a bright beacon shining through the other side.

Now that I look back on my 44 years, I can say with absolute certainty that I've lived a wonderful life. There were many times, throughout, I wouldn't have classified it as such. Sometimes there were sad, lonely, and uninspired days that felt like an eternity. But I am who I am because of them.

Writing this book has been an inspiration to me: a victory, a breakthrough, and a great form of therapy so to speak. I've been able to chronicle my life and dissect it into pieces.

It's been extremely hard at times to be vulnerable, open, and transparent. There have been many moments in my life that have been private and held close to my heart. This was mostly due to the feelings of failure, embarrassment, and shame. I wasn't happy with who I was, and I wanted to be the best. I've always had that mentality, from early childhood sports to my military career. Striving for greatness and being a winner is who I was, until I wasn't. It has been a crazy roller coaster journey over these years, all of it leading up to where I am now.

It came to me in a dream that I should write this book: an epiphany of sorts. It was at this time that I knew I was ready to share my story. It's imperative to know where we are coming from to get to where we're going. I could no longer hide my past. I needed to *"deal to heal.*" It was the right time to share what has worked in my life. There are things that helped me get out of that funk, despair, and turmoil and into a life that's so amazingly awesome. I knew I had some knowledge to share, not as an expert, but as someone who has had the real-life experience of life lessons. Good and bad.

Maybe you're down and out at the moment going through a divorce, job loss, and midlife crisis. It could be anything. I've personally been a part of those as well. It's never too late to add something new to the mix that just might give you back the spark you need to get energized about life. We have a short go on this earth, and we should try to maximize every possible day.

Every day, we're bombarded by all these new buzz words, diets, fads, YouTubers, and news that quite frankly is saddening. Where do we start when we just want to better our lives and nourish our minds?

Well, that's where I come in. I've been working hard reading, listening, and talking to people, friends, and experts out there and putting those things into action.

Hopefully I can help guide you through all this great information, share a few stories, and give you some guidance and insight on what I've gathered over the years. I wanted to combine the best of all the books, podcasts, and life experiences to give you a condensed version of the milestones that had an impact on my life.

After scouring all those resources, I found eight things that I thought were essential to me and could benefit anybody trying to improve their current situation.

In the course of this book, I will go over these eight essential areas that are important to a healthy, loving life full of excitement and riches, and that will help you prosper in whatever you do.

Here's a quick insight into each chapter to come.

Life Distractions: Deciphering the Digital World, Media, and Much More...

For the first chapter, I wanted to lay out the foundation for the rest of the book. We must know where we're coming from if we're going to know where we're going. I'm talking about the distractions and stressors of everyday life. We live in an instant gratification society filled with everything from the internet and cell phone to TV, movies, and fast food – all of it waiting to dissect your mind, body, and soul. I'll tell you what I learned and what you can watch for so that we can all live our most optimal lives.

Step 1: Finding Passion in Your Career

In this chapter, we look at how important it is to have a career that you love, no matter what that career path looks like or how often it turns. If you are going to make a living doing what you hate, how can you possibly find satisfaction in your everyday life? We'll talk about how that transcends relationships and home life. Having found a career or two and the workplace I love, I know you, too, can find solace in waking up and going to work each and every day.

Step 2: Meditation

In this chapter, we're going to explore the essentials of meditation and a few examples of some different methods. But most of all, I'll show you how easy it can be. Meditation was something I had skepticism about when I first started, but it has been a lifesaver every day since. Five minutes a day is all you need. That's it!

Step 3: Reading & Journaling

In this chapter, I'm going to talk about the mindset that you can tap into when you begin to journal your thoughts, feelings, and desires. I'll also talk about the knowledge you'll obtain by reading. Not only have reading and journaling given me an insight about who I am, I've learned more in the past few years than I have in a lifetime of mindless wandering.

Step 4: Relationships

This was an absolute necessity to include, as relationships are so vital to an overall healthy life. We spend hours upon hours with our loved ones. If you can't make that work, then your life will suffer and stall. If we're going to commit to someone, then we need to be 100% all in, always ahead of the game and, as my wife puts it, ABD – Always be dating.

Step 5: Law of Attraction

This was an exciting chapter for me to write. I've done so much reading on this subject over the last few years, and I'm excited to share with you what I've learned. You're in for a great treat. Keep your minds open as the Law of Attraction is real, alive, and available to all of us. I will help break it down and explain how it can benefit *YOU*.

Step 6: Healthy Living

I'm a huge advocate of a healthy living lifestyle. We know how much exercise and food can affect us mentally and physically. We're going to dive into healthy living from that perspective. I'll explain why it's important to be active and how it can help you achieve the best version of you. We will also touch on some diet fads, exercise routines, and the importance of recovery.

Step 7: Gratitude and Blessings

Having gratitude and blessings for life are what make it fun. I'll show you the impact gratitude can have on your daily routine and share with you how being grateful can change your overall health and well-being.

Step 8: Forgiveness and Joy

We as a society have put on so much emotional armour that we're afraid to expose the pain and fears we have. We're so stubborn beyond belief that we've forgotten to forgive others, especially ourselves. If we're to be the best version of ourselves, we have to and must forgive ourselves, period. It's time for you to be vulnerable and open to the joys in your life.

Finding Your Inspiration

In this last chapter, we're going to touch on the reasons we should dream big and never give up, and look at some motivational tools to inspire you. You've worked too hard and put too much time into being present to let life slip by. Let's begin your journey by nourishing your health, mind, and soul.

Tara's Story: Her Life, Her Vision

This chapter is dedicated to my beautiful wife. After knowing her life story and the trial, heartache, and tribulations she's endured, I wanted to share her vision with you. She's extremely knowledgeable when it comes to reading and journaling. Her career intertwines with a healthy lifestyle and this is how she does it.

I hope you enjoy the topics and discussions throughout the book. Whether you take one or even eight things away from this and apply it to your daily life, I know you will find yourself in a better place.

Maybe you practice a few already, or you find you know nothing at all. No worries. Each chapter is an introduction or reminder of how powerful learning about and growing our minds and bodies can be if we want to take full advantage of our lives. Just remember you're on a fantastic ride called life, and it should be as enjoyable as possible.

I have included challenges and checklists at the end of each chapter. Hopefully, they help kick-start your mental and physical game to a whole new level. These steps have helped me get to a place where I can genuinely say I'm grateful for all I have and all I've learned. I continually strive to be better for myself, my wife, my daughter, and our family.

I'm so excited to share them with you. Don't forget to have fun along the way!!

Add up all your little steps and BIG things will happen

~ JS

LIFE DISTRACTIONS:

Deciphering the Digital World, Media, and Much More...

First off, I would like to thank you for joining me on this journey. I hope after reading this book you have a little more clarity and direction on what it takes to find your strength, inner peace, and true happiness. We'll start with what has brought me to this point in my life.

It's hard to believe it's been over 26 years since I ventured away from home to join the military. I've lived in multiple states, endured two failed marriages, and eventually settled down in Nova Scotia, Canada. It seems like it was just yesterday.

Forty-four years on this earth and I have a beautiful life. I wouldn't trade it for the world.

Today I'm in an awesome, loving relationship with an amazing woman and I have family that supports me with love and inspires me to be the best version of me.

Unfortunately this wasn't always the case. I've had many days of feeling worthless and lacking motivation, and thinking countless thoughts about how I had let so many people down.

After failing my second marriage, I sat and pondered what my life was about to look like. Twice divorced, having a split family, and not knowing what was lying ahead, I knew I had to do something drastic to set my path in a positive direction.

After my first divorce, I had crashed hard. I was in a horrible state of depression and living in a new city without a network of friends and family. Things had spiralled far out of control. I was at the lowest point in my life. Absolute rock bottom. I had been young and I'd had the world in my hands, and all within several weeks it felt like it had been snatched out of thin air.

So after my second divorce, I wanted a sign from the universe that things were going to get better. That sign ended up being in multiple forms. It started with an incredible career that was on the rise, and a healthy lifestyle change which included fueling my body properly. It also included a total submersion into my local CrossFit affiliate. Reading now became a priority, as well as my morning journaling. I was engulfed in my new-found love of meditation.

Lastly, the best sign came from my gorgeous wife. I've shed many tears getting things off my chest. She has been there and listened when I needed it most. I'm grateful for her enduring love and what she brought to our relationship.

Things really took a turn for the best when I started journaling about my life. As I journaled, it became more evident that maybe I did have something to share. I thought that if I could transcend all the things that have helped me and combine them into one book, perhaps I could help others find that amazing life that awaits them.

My hope is that after reading through the chapters you will begin your own life full of joy, gratitude, and happiness. We live in ever-changing times. There is so much abundance in the world; you just have to ask the universe for what you want.

Finding Your Way

Maybe your situation is similar to mine; or perhaps life has just thrown you a curveball, as it will from time to time. We need something to rely on physically, mentally, and spiritually to help us get back.

Life can be messy, and I want to help you get back on track to what I believe we're on this planet to do; to enjoy and embrace the love around us. I wish I'd had this information at my fingertips when I was young and impressionable

Like most people, we work eight hours a day, spend time taking the kids to practice, and somewhere in between get a few moments to ourselves. How do we know what to do when it comes to finding our own identity and inner peace?

Let's take a look at a few things I think are responsible for throwing you daily distractions and sending you on your way to Negativity-Ville. These are high on the list of things I believe are responsible for compromising your love for yourself and others, as well as putting you in a state of low vibration. We need to be cautious and alert as we navigate through them.

If we're to live our best version of ourselves, we need to be in a constant state of high frequency. Let's get to it!

Digital Media

Where do we start? What can we possibly do? Digital media has become the new norm. It's what has come to define our lives. Ever have those days where you're online for hours, travelling down the endless rabbit hole that is the internet, all on the quest to find something that might spark your interest or catch your eye? You might read an article or two, watch your favourite YouTube channel, or get caught up on social media. This usually ends up leaving you with an empty void and mental fatigue. I've been there and done that and it's exhausting. I want to help you navigate through all the B.S. in the hopes of nourishing your health, mind, and soul.

Ok, before we get to all the uplifting ways to improve the Mind, Body, and Soul, we first need to find out what it is that distracts us from reaching our goals and dreams.

We're living in a digital age. Everything we need or want is at our fingertips, all from the comfort and convenience of our digital devices. It's said, *"The average American spends 5.4 hours a day on their phone. Millennials spend slightly more time on their phones (5.7 hours) compared to baby boomers (5 hours) on average." Ref 1*

Those are quite staggering numbers once you factor in the typical workday. How much time is left to spend with your friends, family, and loved ones? We're going to dive into a variety of topics, most of which are related to the smart phone, social media, and the internet.

I promise you I won't be on a soapbox about how the digital world has taken away our personal space and social interaction with others. On the contrary, I love today's technology. I enjoy watching TV and Movies and surfing the internet as much as the next person. Believe it or not, I wrote this book on my phone. That's amazingly convenient: not having to carry around a clunky laptop and being able to write any time an idea popped into my head. (Yes, I was the guy at Starbucks with his head buried in his phone.)

As a so-called generation Xer, I got caught in the middle of old and new technology. The *"Old"* you might remember was the telephone attached to the wall, the beeper, and dial-up modems. Then there's the *"New"* consisting of the highly advanced smart phone with its endless possibilities. With its countless resources and endless information, the smart phone single-handedly rendered my Encyclopedia Britannica collection useless. You fellow Xers know what I'm talking about. I admit: falling in between technological generations has been a giant learning curve. I have grown fond of the simplicity of current technology. It has made life simpler and convenient. But it is also confusing and overwhelming.

Here's the knock-on that. With all this technology and media in our face 24 hours a day, we need to be aware of the pitfalls. Around every corner, something is lurking ready to distract you from your true potential. I'm here to enlighten you and remind you why we need to be mindful of everything around you.

Social Media - Love It or Hate It. We're Stuck With It

With the greatness that is social media, I've come to the conclusion that for better or worse we're stuck with it. It's taken me a while to adjust to the onslaught of posts that I receive daily. However, how great is it that we're able to connect in an instant with friends and family. We can follow their lives as they get married, have kids and take trips to amazing places.

Here's the rub on that. With all the greatness of it, we can also drive ourselves batty as we compare and adjust our lives according to what we see online. Insecurity, embarrassment and shame can grab hold of us if we let it.

Many nights I've caught myself falling into that trap, looking at Facebook and Instagram and wondering how it is that all my friends have this perfect life portrayed for all to see. I mean, did I miss the memo on this? I'm twice divorced, and it seems like everyone else has the perfect family life.

Well, I have some news for you. What you see is only a glimpse of what people are going through – the so-called best of the best. Don't fall into the trap so common in our society and believe everything you see. We, as humans, crave acknowledgement and respect from our peers. It's only natural that you are going to see sun-soaked vacations, Disneyland trips, and beautiful engagements. It's probably the 1% of a life you see. There's a whole other 99% kept behind closed doors.

Good or bad, social media is out there, and we need to navigate through it carefully, knowing this. I'm not knocking social media. After all, I met my beautiful wife online, so I know it can be amazing! If we can see social media for what it is, I believe we can use it for good. What we don't need are all these mental distractions that have completely zapped our love for ourselves and others. Your life is wonderful and full of endless possibilities.

Television (TV)

I've always been a massive fan of comedy. You know those shows where you're bent over, belly hurts from laughing, tears rolling down your face? It really is the kind of medicine that nourishes the soul.

It's said that laughing releases endorphins from your brain, reduces the level of stress in your body, and strengthens the immune system. We know that laughter therapy, also known as humour therapy, can reduce negativity, emotional stress, and physical discomfort. These are some great positive mental and physical aspects to watching comedy on TV. Unfortunately, for every positive step forward we're bombarded by the multitude of negative side effects. Excessive TV-watching (more than three hours a day) can contribute to sleep difficulties, behaviour problems, lower grades, and other health issues to name a few.

So I'm not against TV-watching as an activity. My point about today's television is that it's been entirely oversaturated. We live in an age of society with too many choices surrounding our television and movie channels – so much so that I believe we have gotten to the point where we've become social introverts. We've completely closed ourselves off from the world, and decided that the comfort of pyjamas and a bag of chips is going to win out.

Don't get me wrong. I'm not saying there's anything wrong with channel surfing for the newest series or the latest movies. But it can be easy to get distracted from the important things in life after spending a day binge-watching the last two seasons of your favourite show.

I read an article recently that stated *"too much sitting, especially when watching television can be bad for your health, research suggests. It has been linked to diseases such as diabetes and cancer. It also has been tied to an increased risk of mental health issues, such as anxiety and depression." Ref 2*

I think we're all very aware of this couch potato theory. So for the sake of our well-being, let's just limit our time on the tube. Have a talk with a loved one, pick up a book, or go for a walk instead; if not only for your own sanity, do it for your health.

Gossip Magazines

Although the magazine industry is dying, we still see it around. If you've been in a grocery store in the past 20 years, you know what I'm talking about. The magazines are next to the candy and gum at the checkout line. Ever notice all those magazine covers depicting the latest workout craze, diet or even which celebrity is divorcing who this month?

These magazines have been around forever, and although they can be entertaining and funny, they don't serve much of a purpose other than to fill our minds with nonsense; they're gossip magazines for a reason. It's gossip, and a lot of that information is related to body image, dating advice, and outright lies. It's no wonder our perception of what's real is skewed.

In 2019 my wife and I went to Mexico for a week. While we were waiting at the airport, she mentioned that it would be fun if we read some *"trashy magazines"* while we were on the beach. She must have known I didn't understand what she was talking about by the look on my face. She then proceeded to pick one up from the rack, with what I assume was one of the Jonas brothers. I got a good chuckle and said yes, let's get one.

It was an entertaining read. We both laughed on the beach as we got exactly what we had expected: articles filled with gossip. It was probably the first trashy magazine I had read in 10 plus years and most likely the last. Just know that if you decide to read one, take the information with a grain of salt and realize it's strictly there for entertainment purposes.

News

My memories stem back to my childhood, sitting on the couch watching the local 6 p.m. news with my parents while eating our TV dinners. I don't remember too much, but the things I do recall were always related to some sort of tragedy.

There are many horrible situations that happen in the world, and people should know about these things through the news channels. These bad things include crime, famine, wars, violence, political views, and injustice. I can still recall the Challenger shuttle explosion or the LA riots, and the massive San Francisco earthquake in 1989.

These things still resonate with me today. They were horrific events in our history, and I'm sad for all those involved. They were newsworthy events that were captured by some brave people.

But in between those catastrophes, there was a tendency – and it's a growing trend – to overemphasize day-to-day events in the world. One study even suggests that *"Participants who watched the negatively valenced bulletin showed increases in both anxious and sad mood, and also showed a significant increase in the tendency to catastrophize a personal worry." Ref 3*

"Those results are consistent with those theories of worry that implicate negative mood as a causal factor in facilitating worrisome thought. They also suggest that negatively valenced T.V. news programs can exacerbate a range of personal concerns that are not specifically relevant to the content of the program."
Ref 4

After hearing all that, it's no wonder we're living in a constant state of fear. It's your job to learn and grasp the reality of today's TV news, determining what's of value and what might be propaganda. Again, it's just about being aware and moderated.

Texting

Wow! Where do I start with this one? This is a pet peeve of mine. Close your eyes and picture this: you're on a date with your significant other, and you're about to be seated. As you make your way to the table, you look around and notice a couple in the corner booth waiting for their dinner to be served. Both are hunched over looking at their phones. Nearby, a massive company party seems to be alive and vibrant, but half the group is engaged on their phones, texting or posting about how great the dinner was. It's impressive really how texting has changed the linguistic landscape for better or worse.

A recent article stated that *"texting hinders all types of communication including, written, face-to-face, and surface level. It also causes problems with social boundaries and worsens our impatience and need for instant gratification. It states that texting takes away from building social confidence skills and the need for meaningful conversations. It also says that we get so used to writing in 'slang', that it may start to appear in our formal writing." Ref 5*

There isn't a day goes by that I don't see someone's head buried in their phone (me included) texting a friend, loved one, or co-worker.

The health aspects of texting alone make it worth taking a break from time to time. Here are a few that have impacted me. I've been guilty of all of them.

Blue Light Emission - I've suffered many restless nights binge-watching the latest series or texting into the late-night hours. In a recent study out of Harvard it stated, *"While light of any kind can suppress the secretion of melatonin, blue light at night does so more powerfully. Harvard researchers and their colleagues conducted an experiment comparing the effects of 6.5 hours of exposure to blue light to exposure to green light of comparable brightness. The blue light suppressed melatonin for about twice as long as the green light and shifted circadian rhythms by twice as much (3 hours vs. 1.5 hours)." Ref 6*

If that's not enough to convince you to put the phone away at night and get some much-needed rest, I don't know what is.

Texting and Driving - Doesn't this seem like a no brainer? We've all seen that person racing down the highway, drifting from lane to lane, only to pull up beside them and see their head down, eyes on their phone. Listen, I've been guilty of checking my phone while driving. Most have and it's not worth it.

I've made it a point in the past few years to always use my Bluetooth in the car and turn off the phone messages when I'm driving. Way too many people have been injured or lost their lives because they took that five-second glance at their phone only to lose sight of where they were.

It's been stated that *"Using a cell phone use while driving, whether it's hand-held or hands-free, delays a driver's reactions as much as having a blood alcohol concentration at the legal limit of .08 percent and is six times more likely to cause a car accident than drunk driving." Ref 48*

These are scary statistics. It should be a lesson to all of us.

Work and School Suffers - I still remember the day when I graduated from the flip phone to my fancy new iPhone. I didn't realize at the time, but the new-found technology and startup of social media sites soon consumed countless hours of my day. It was time I couldn't get back.

Nowadays, whether I'm on the phone for work or checking in with friends and family, I'm always aware of the time spent, and I monitor it with the best intentions. It's so easy these days to be immersed in a project at work or cramming for an exam only to get that dreaded ding on the phone. Next thing you know you're caught in a conversation, only to return to the work at hand 30 minutes later.

This scenario came back to haunt me at a previous job. I was working on a project with a sensitive deadline. During the day, I had received a text from an "ex" only to start engaging in a text war that continued for the next two hours. All out of sorts and mad as hell, I had a hard time concentrating on the task at hand. I completely lost sight of my deadline. A few days later my manager had a chat with me about not getting the work done on time. I was lucky enough to get an extra day to finish; and I did. The talking to was enough for me to straighten up.

We live in a time when our cellphones are a primary source of communication. Let's be mindful of the time we spend using them.

Relationships, Friends, Family - Texting can be a great source of communication. It's something I use daily in my job and personal life. As great as it is, we need to be aware of the people in our present moment.

I've been in situations where texting hindered that personal moment. You can probably picture that moment talking to a friend or co-worker only for them to answer a text and get back to you with, *"ok, where were we."* Sort of kills the moment, doesn't it?

Or maybe you're on a date only to have the other person respond to a text. If you're like me, you're wondering what's more important to them at this moment. Are they trying to get out of here? Maybe they don't like me.

One of the things my wife and I practice is putting our phones away on date night. If someone needs to reach us in an emergency, they'll call. This allows me to give her my full attention, and we're able to enjoy our quality time together. Give it a try. It's quite liberating.

Posture - Ever notice how your neck hurts after being on the phone for hours? I know I have, and it doesn't feel great. It might be advantageous to take a break and stretch out a bit before heading back to your texting marathon. *"Text neck describes a repetitive stress injury or overuse syndrome in the neck, caused by prolonged use of mobile devices with the head bent downward and not moving."* Ref 43

This is one of many physical issues brought about by the rise of the cell phone. Maybe if we limit our time online, have more face-to-face conversations, and possibly use the phone feature to talk, we'll not only have better posture, but we'll start to feel that physical interaction that is human connection.

Final Thoughts

Ok, so we laid it all out there in this chapter. We talked about the entanglements that today's society presents. We mentioned everything from social media and news to cell phones. We also covered how easy it can be to get tangled in a web of distractions if we aren't present and aware of the moment. I'm no stranger to any of them, and as your habits change, you'll probably wonder how we could have been so careless as to let distractions dictate our lives in the first place.

I want to leave you with a worksheet I'm calling *"Unplugged."* I want to challenge you to endure one week with as minimal distractions as possible. It will give you a chance to reset and focus on other areas of your life. Give it a shot! You have nothing to lose. It's your time; own it! Head over to healthmindsoul.com and download your copy.

Going offline becomes
a peace of mind

~ JS

Unplugged

"I challenge myself to a digital detox for one week"

1. List 3 things you will minimize this week.
Ex: TV, news, social media

A. _____

B. _____

C. _____

2. List 3 things you'll replace your distractions with.
Ex: reading, exercise, journaling

A. _____

B. _____

C. _____

3. I will put my phone away at _____p.m.

4. Tips for a successful detox.

A. Work with someone else if possible. Accountability is key.

B. Most phones have usage hours. Check the hours before the week and after.

C. Ask yourself *"why?"* each time you pull out your phone.

STEP 1

Finding Passion in Your Career

I've always felt enthusiastic about my work, so much so that I wanted to write about the importance of finding that passion in your career. I know from personal experience how important it's been to my physical and mental health. Being enthusiastic about my work has also given me the ability to see the bright lights when everything seemed so glum. When previous relationships started to suffer, the one constant was my ability to lean on my co-workers. Having that amazing workplace was a constant reminder of how great my life was despite my own personal struggles.

Don't get me wrong, I'm not saying that once you've found that magical career you have been searching for, then everything will be perfect. What I do know is that it can be comforting knowing you have another outlet outside of your friends and family to count on. You can never have too much support.

I found a few interesting stats I thought were important to share before we went any further: it's said, *"The average person spends more than 90,000 hours in their lifetime at work, and it affects their personal lives. Also, an astounding 87% of Americans have no passion for their jobs, and a quarter of them say that work is their number one stress." Ref 8* Yikes!! So convert those hours to years, and lo and behold that works out to 10 years of our lives on earth spent with little to no passion and massive stress. That seems like a disaster waiting to happen.

The most important reason you should do what you love is, simply and honestly, to feel happy each and every day. You have fantastic opportunities presented to you when you least expect it, and life is too short to be stuck in a place that you don't feel passionate about.

Yes, I've had to endure trying times and sacrifice the job for happiness, but you can bet when the time was right, I ventured out into something new. Was it terrifying? Absolutely. There are going to be many monumental moments in your life pursuing new careers and opportunities.

I know firsthand what a wild ride life can be and my career was no different. I thought life was going to be simple if I just planned it out right. I pictured it being just like the books, TV, and college brochures showed. I assumed I would go to university, find a job, and hopefully, if all went well, enjoy a rewarding 30-year career. Maybe if it all went just right, I'd collect a steady paycheck and a pension. Sounds great, doesn't it? Well, for the majority of us, life rarely ends up like that.

Career Journey

My work journey started early in life. Somewhere around the age of 13, I began cutting grass with my dad. I spent countless summers and holidays making great money as a teenager. While most of my friends were still getting allowance, I was hoarding stacks of 20-dollar bills. Of course making that money had its price. Don't get me wrong, working with my dad and spending time together was great, but I wanted my summers free to hang out with my buddies, or to sleep in. That was an awakening moment when I knew money wasn't everything for me, and having a job that makes me happy was. Quite the epiphany for a teenager, don't you think?

For me, I started my post-secondary education right out of high school at the local Junior College. I wasn't but a semester in when I knew I wasn't going to enjoy the rigours of school life. After some serious soul searching, I decided I was going to enlist in the U.S. Navy. This is where I enlisted as a hospital corpsman and eventually went on to pursue my Biomedical Technology Certification.

I spent some amazing years in the Navy on land and at sea. I even had the opportunity of deployment to Iraq. After having spent 10 years in the Navy, I felt it was time to find something new that would drive my passion for work and life.

Although I contemplated staying in longer, it wasn't in my heart, and I didn't have the drive to sustain another 10 years. After my last tour was up, I was honorably discharged.

At that point, for whatever reason, I felt the need to leave California. I consulted with my family and drove from California to Austin, Texas. I had little money and no job in hand. It was crazy, looking back on it. I had packed up all my belongings and even rented a home in the hopes I would land that perfect career. It's a damn good thing I landed the job, because I hadn't even considered having a backup plan.

What I thought was going to be an amazing job and life in Austin unfortunately came to a crashing halt a year later as I was filing for divorce and looking for a new job. Neither were working out.

It was by sheer luck that my girlfriend at the time, who by the way was living in Nova Scotia, Canada, mentioned that a job opening had been posted for a Biomedical Technologist at the children's hospital in Halifax. Admittedly, even thinking about moving was nuts, right. I mean California to Texas was crazy enough for me. Now a whole new country.

Canada, Eh! Here I was, 1000s of miles east with no family and a new job. Luckily for me I found my dream job. I'm still at the same hospital loving every moment and *"Living the Dream."* I've now been in Halifax for the last decade plus. It's literally the best job I've ever held. I love the people, and the flexibility I have working and balancing my family life is incredible. Is it challenging? Yes. Can it be stressful? Yes. But what I know is every day I'm excited about what tests and challenges are thrown my way. I wouldn't want to be anywhere else.

Over the course of 20 years I've had an array of careers and jobs that somehow, some way, led me to where I am now. You might find the *"you're perfect"* job on the first go-round. You might have to wait years like I did. But you will find it. Your perfect career is out there waiting for you.

When you do find it, like anything else, you're going to have to work at keeping that passion. Here are a few things I've found that helped me and will help you find and maintain joy and happiness in the work you do.

Self-Esteem - Have you ever had a moment where you're being rewarded for a job well done? Maybe it's through a promotion, pay raise or congratulations from a colleague. It's that feeling you get when you know the hard work has paid off and you're finally being recognized. At this point self-esteem is at an all-time high. Don't we all love that? That self-esteem is possible once you've discovered the job you are passionate about.

Having that passion is what drives performance and allows you to go above and beyond what's required.

It lets you be decisive and mission-oriented. These are things that get noticed and have helped me achieve success. Here are a few benefits of high self-esteem.

"Employees who have a high level of self-esteem will trust their thinking and judgement and are therefore likely to make better decisions. Having these qualities also enables us to create more effective interpersonal and work relationships which means that we can more effectively contribute to the work environment around us. As leaders, high levels of self esteem mean we are able to focus more positively on other people and their development, rather than spend time berating our own performance." Ref 9

Healthy Work Environment - Don't we all want to have our health and be able to live a happy, productive life? Sure we do. Having a healthy work environment can improve employee productivity in several ways. First, healthy employees feel better, have more energy and endurance, and are more capable of working hard at their jobs.

Second, a healthy work environment can contribute to employee happiness. Companies that value their employees tend to treat them with respect and value their opinions. If employees feel appreciated by their employers, they are more likely to like their jobs and feel happy at work.

I read an article recently that pointed out some particular health benefits of happy workers.

"By keeping a healthy work environment, you keep your employees healthy as well. They will have more energy and endurance. You can expect them to think faster, work more, and feel less fatigued.

Next, an employee's mental wellbeing. People will feel better, and they will be more motivated to get their work done. They will have better morale, and may even have better creativity. A positive work environment means people will be more prepared to take on risks, which can give you amazing returns if they pan out." *Ref 10*

Deep down, we all care about our health and longevity. A healthy workplace is one area we can benefit from.

Motivation – In the workforce these days, it's imperative to find reasons to be productive. Loving your career should be one of them.

"Studies show that happy employees are 12% more productive than unhappy employees. Imagine what would happen if your company's entire workforce increased its productivity by 12%!" Ref 11

There's nothing more frustrating than having a lack of motivation. I would assume this applies to all aspects of life. Think about it: if you had to wake up each day dreading the thought of going to work, I'm positive you would pack it in and look for something else.

I've been on both extremes of the motivation pendulum, and it can change ever so fast. Lose track of what is going on in your job, and you could be left with your head spinning.

There's only one true way for you to motivate yourself to work hard: don't think of it as hard work. You should think of it as moulding yourself into the person you want to be. When you've made the choice to get after it, try not to think about how difficult or unthinkable it might be; just think about how amazing it must be, or how proud you might feel to have done that. We all have it inside us. Now go out and make it look easy.

Motivation is essential for innovation. I believe it's also necessary for achieving your career goals, crucial for allowing good habits to flow, and extremely vital to becoming successful in life.

Finding a passion for work will drive that motivation through the roof! Don't be surprised when good things happen from working at a job you love.

I love my career and what I do. Most days, I'm on point and checking things off the to-do list; other days, it's tough even to finish an email. We continuously need something that gives us the motivation to produce – loving your career, the money, the freedom.

Whenever I'm in a rut or can't find that drive, I think about when I was stationed at Marine Corps Base Camp Pendleton. I was over a year into my tour there. Work in the shop crept along at its usual pace until that dreaded day that was forever known as 9/11. That's when things took a turn for the worse.

I still remember the day like it was yesterday. It was Sep 11, 2001. The attacks on the World Trade Center were being reported. I headed to work in a frenzy and was devastated by what I had seen on TV. Everyone on base was distraught, and things were looking grim. You could feel the sadness in the room.

As the days and weeks went by, the troops started to rally in anticipation of the possibility of war. Our battalion gathered together and put on what can only be construed as a fire so hot and ready to burn. We were motivated. We came together as a cohesive team and worked extremely hard over the following few months to get things ready for what was soon to be a deployment overseas. I'm proud to have been a part of something so grand and patriotic.

I've never seen such a rise in productivity in my life since. I do know, after seeing all that, that we have that capability as people to rally together no matter what job or circumstance arises. I believe there are no limits to what we can accomplish when we're that motivated. If you have something like that to reflect on in your own life, take that as a reminder of how amazing things can be.

Final Thoughts

It doesn't matter what career path you choose or how you get there. It doesn't matter how much you make, whether you have many co-workers, or have a career as a solo entrepreneur. It's about loving your job, loving your life, and knowing you serve a deeper purpose than your own.

As we venture out into the world and grow wiser, our tastes for what we want in life changes. It's fantastic to have dreams and pursue them. It is what our ultimate goal is here, finding that career you love

I've provided a checklist for your current work journey. It's a chance to see what you love, or to reflect on things that you would like to change. Have fun and get to know what it is that makes you happy! Head over to healthmindsoul.com and download your copy.

Once you've found passion in your career, work becomes a thing of the past

~ JS

Career Journey

On a scale of 1-10. How would you rate your career? _____

1. List 3 things you love about your career

    A. _____

    B. _____

    C. _____

2. List 3 things you dislike about your career

    A. _____

    B. _____

    C. _____

3. What would your dream job – career – look like?

_____

_____

4. What can you do in your current career to make it something you can be passionate about?

_____

_____

_____

STEP 2

Meditation

It's 6 a.m. and the morning sun has started to come over the horizon. I can hear my heartbeat as I start to slow my breathing. I take in a few deep breaths as I listen to the birds outside the window. My body is gradually falling into a relaxed state. I have my legs draped over the bed, hand in my lap, and my mind is venturing into a spiritual state of acceptance, ready to receive.

I begin to feel how grateful I am for the day ahead; my mind is starting to fill with joy and love. I slowly map out the day, from the drive into work until I'm lying in bed at night. As I'm professing all the great things that will happen throughout the day, I finish with a few affirmations and mantras. This kick-starts the day, leaving me full of passion and excitement.

This has become my morning ritual for the last few years, something I practice every day. The best part about it: I can do it all in 10 minutes and so can you! I've made it a priority every morning to begin with an accepting mind and open heart, ready to tackle whatever is thrown my way.

Later on I'll talk about the importance of exercise and food on the body. It's equally – if not more – important to train your so-called *"Spiritual Muscle."* That's right, believe it or not, your brain is your spiritual muscle. Your mind needs a daily workout regime too, and not from the likes of the TV or the internet, but from genuine spiritual consciousness, like meditation and mindfulness.

If it's not something you practice already, you're probably asking yourself, what is it? How will it help me? To answer the first part:

Meditation is as old as time; we're talking somewhere around 3,500 years old. It's a practice that has withstood the test of time only to regain popularity in what I believe to be the most existential period of self-consciousness and awareness.

Meditation is described as *"a practice where an individual uses a technique – such as mindfulness, or focusing the mind on a particular object, thought, or activity – to train attention and awareness, and achieve a mentally clear and emotionally calm and stable state." Ref 46*

I will admit to being a skeptic when it came to the practice of meditation and mindfulness. It has taken me a while to warm up to the idea of clearing my mind of clutter and filling it with thoughts of joy, gratitude, and love. I want you to enjoy the same awareness and feelings I get from it on a daily basis.

Here are a few thoughts you might have about making a commitment to practicing meditation. I had those thoughts too.

Thought #1

I don't have enough time in my already busy day. I have to get out the door to work, get my kids ready for school, lunches made, and still find time for myself.

Answer – You will find the time. We all have 5-10 minutes a day to spare. Maybe you make it the first or last thing you do in the day. Whatever time you choose, stick to it, and make it your new habit. Keep at it for a minimum of five minutes. If you feel inclined to go longer once you've gotten better, go for it!

Thought # 2

How can I possibly sit still for 5-10 minutes when my mind is wandering all over the place?

Answer – It's ok! You don't necessarily need to sit in a state of silence. Just find a beautiful quiet place and let your thoughts flow. Listen to the sounds of nature. If there's a particular song that makes you feel good, try it. Meditation is about listening to your thoughts and being accepting of them. It's taking control of those thoughts and being mindful of each one.

Thought # 3

Isn't meditation only for those that are gurus, you know the ones you see online sitting crossed legged and chanting their mantras?

Answer – Absolutely not! Nowadays, you'll have CEOs and executives, professional athletes, and entertainers embracing meditation as a way to reconnect with oneself, and so can *YOU*!

Just as a professional athlete doesn't perfect their skills overnight, neither will you. It is a lifelong commitment. It takes time and practice.

Thought # 4

How can this possibly make me a better person in both body and mind?

Answer – There is so much overwhelming data and research on this subject. I've read so many articles and journals on the merits of meditation on the body and mind, I was instantly sold. It's literally 5-10 minutes a day, and it's free. Who doesn't like free? Time is the only cost. Let me tell you, it's worth it.

I've referenced some scientifically backed research that shows you 12 reasons alone to access the positive benefits of meditation.

"Reduced stress

Control anxiety

Promotes emotional health

Enhances self-awareness

Lengthens attention span

May reduce age-related memory loss

Can generate kindness

Help fight addictions

Improve sleep

Control pain

Decrease blood pressure

Ability to meditate anywhere"

Ref 12

This is outstanding. I love research, and seeing these benefits really fires me up. It gets me more motivated to become mindful and aware of my thoughts and feelings.

Meditation Journey

For me, meditation has helped me become more focused, relaxed, and just plain more grateful than I ever thought possible. I struggle all the time and have a long way to go. Meditation is a great place to start and I now have a blueprint to understanding my thoughts and being present in the moment. It is so liberating.

Think about it: as humans we have, on average, 50,000 thoughts a day, mostly unconscious. Ever wonder how you drove to work and arrived as if you weren't even there. That's the unconscious mind working its magic. If somehow we can be in control of a significant percentage of our thoughts by practicing meditation, then I'm willing to give it a *try*.

"95 percent of brain activity is beyond our conscious awareness. Numerous cognitive neuroscientists have conducted studies that have revealed that only 5% of our cognitive activities (decisions, emotions, actions, behaviour) is conscious whereas the remaining 95% is generated in a non-conscious manner." Ref 13

Give yourself that 10 minutes a day, setting a time, and making it a habit. It will then become a new ritual you can't live without. It will put you in a great mindset before the day's hustle and bustle. If you are already a practicing meditator, kudos to you, you are ahead of the game. Keep up the amazing work. If you're like

most people out there, it's probably something new –
most likely with a tinge of skepticism.

As we continue through this section, we will cover the
basics of meditation and where to start. I won't leave
you hanging, I promise. Here are a few things you can
build upon and some great information to help with
your mindfulness and awareness practices.

Meditation 101

Meditate for 5-10 Minutes - It might seem like an eternity
in the beginning. Sitting and consciously listening to
one's thoughts isn't something we're used to doing.
I recommend having your phone handy and set the
timer for five minutes. The last thing you want to be
doing is opening your eyes to check the time regularly.

You want to get into a high state of mind here. If you're
using your phone, don't forget to turn it to airplane
mode. Numerous dings, incoming messages, and texts
are just going to distract you further or possibly outright
stop you. I feel empowered when I shut my phone
down. It puts me in a state of acceptance, and I know
it's *"My Time."* After all, our objective is to connect to
a part of ourselves through our thoughts and mind. If
you're worried about what's going on in the other room
or who might be calling, you then start to defeat the
purpose.

Start with your five-minute meditation practice. Once
you feel comfortable, slowly begin to increase it by a
minute or two. Before you know it, you'll be on your way
to 10 minutes.

Finding Your Perfect Time to Meditate - I don't believe that the time of day has to be set in stone. Maybe you're not a morning person, or you enjoy finishing your day with a relaxing mindfulness session. The key is trying to be consistent and find a time that suits you. Remember, you want this to turn into a daily habit, something that you can make permanent over time.

I love doing my meditation first thing in the morning, as I find my mind is the most transparent and awake then. I have no distractions from the hectic day, and it helps to put me in a high state of mind.

Another reason I do it early – and probably the most important – is so I don't forget. If you do it first thing in the morning you're guaranteed to follow through. You don't want to start a pattern of making excuses. It has caught me in the past, and before I knew it, I had let a week slip by without doing any meditation. The key is to find a time that's right for you. Let's make this a sustainable habit.

Keeping It Simple – Don't worry if you're doing it right. *"Your Way"* will be the right way. Most people tend to get caught up in the 5 Ws – Who, What, When, Where, and Why; things like: do I have the right posture? Am I sitting in the correct position? Am I saying the right things? Let's just start by finding a comfortable place to rest; remember it's only five minutes. Even if all you do is sit and think, that's great. It's a start. You'll have all the time in the world to worry about expanding your daily meditation practice. Each day you'll be gaining knowledge of different methods and techniques that suit your style. It's not a one-size-fits-all routine.

I've personally changed my morning routine many times. Usually I find something interesting in a book or on a podcast; I then take that info, add it to my routine, and see if it sticks. Some things have stayed, and a lot has not. We all have a different way of approaching our mindfulness practice. As you get better, you'll find what suits you.

Control Your Breathing - I've found this to be instrumental in my practice. It is usually the first thing I start with as it gets me into a relaxed, calm, and mindful place.

Begin with your normal breaths. Nothing too long or too short. Start to notice where you feel the breath in your body. Feel the breath through the nostrils to the abdomen. Notice how your chest feels as it expands and collapses ever so slowly. Listen to the sound you make with each breath. I like to start with a finger pressed on one side of my nose and switch nostrils with each breath.

I currently use the 5/5 technique. The 5/5 method is a breathing exercise where you breathe in for a count of five seconds and out for a count of five seconds. It is used to help you relax and regain composure in a variety of situations. I like that I can slow my breathing down before I dive into my daily affirmations and mantras. You will soon find the pattern that suits you.

Don't Worry If Your Thoughts Get Lost - It might not feel comfortable at the beginning; it surely wasn't for me. I would sit there in silence, wondering what I should do next. A wandering mind is ok. Seriously, we conjure up 50,000 thoughts a day. It's no wonder our minds are like a five-lane express highway during rush hour. The key to this is to be mindful of those thoughts and slowly come work your way back. It might be through a breathing technique or affirmation.

To this day, my mind wanders often. I too thought that there was no way I could completely shut this down for the next 5-10 minutes. Some people are amazing at shutting off, and others are a minefield of thoughts about to explode. I've had times where I couldn't stop thinking about a project at work, tasks around the house, or family issues.

The best part is when we become mindful that our thoughts are wandering; this is when we are starting to learn awareness. Awareness is the ability to relate to our ideas and not run away from them. We can then start to listen to stories our minds are telling us. With time, we can train ourselves to see what our habits are. Whether we like them or not, this gives us insight into our minds. We start to learn about ourselves.

When my mind ventures off, I want to take the thoughts that arise – no matter where I'm at in my session – address the idea with gratitude, and ask for help from the universe. I find this is an easy trick to find focus and get back on track.

Practice Gratitude - Gratitude is defined as *"the quality of being thankful; readiness to show appreciation for and to return kindness." Ref 14* Those are some pretty powerful words. We're going to be taking a deeper dive into this subject in a later chapter, as I believe there are so many benefits to the practice of gratitude and appreciation.

Well, why talk about it now then, you ask? The answer is: meditation is a fantastic time to practice gratitude as our minds are vibrating at an extremely high frequency and we're full of thoughts and ideas.

Every morning I begin my meditation with appreciation and gratitude for five things I'm thankful for. This is after I've already journaled five things I'm grateful for. The more places you can infiltrate gratitude into your life, the better you'll feel.

Don't worry, I promise you, you won't run out of things to be thankful for. You might start with being grateful for your health and well-being, the love your family has for you, the morning coffee you drank, or your car being finely tuned. There are no shortages here. Be grateful for whatever comes to mind. This practice will put you in a positive state of mind. Here are a few benefits of gratitude.

"Gratitude is strongly and consistently associated with greater happiness. Gratitude helps people feel more positive emotions, relish good experiences, improve their health, deal with adversity, and build strong relationships. People feel and express gratitude in multiple ways." Ref 15

Mantras and Affirmations

Both Mantras and Affirmations are things that I have recently incorporated into my morning ritual. I don't always use them both. It could be one or the other depending on how my mind is flowing that day, but I do think they both have their place in meditation. They are great at reaffirming our relationship with ourselves.

"A mantra is a sacred utterance, a numinous sound, syllable, word or phonemes, or group of words in Sanskrit believed by practitioners to have mental and spiritual powers." Ref 49

You might be thinking of a mantra as someone chanting or humming loudly and repeatedly, and you would probably be correct. The fact is there are many types of mantras available. They are meant to guide you into a state of enhanced concentration. Here are a few you can use in your daily routine.

Daily mantras:

I will live my most optimal life!
ABD - Always be Dating
I will let the universe show me the way
Thank you for my health and vitality
I love my career and am thankful
for the money I make
I will not let my fears define me
I am grateful and blessed with my life
Meditation has improved my health mind and soul

You can repeat them silently every morning and even have them copied on your phone to repeat throughout the day if you so desire. There are countless other mantras available. If you don't find something you like, feel free to come up with your own. It's *"Your Time, Your Mind."*

Affirmations are great as well. It's a time to reflect on the great person you are and the people in your life.

"Affirmations are positive statements that can help you to overcome negative thoughts. When you repeat them often and believe in them, you can start to make positive changes." Ref 16

How amazing is that? Repeatedly telling yourself how awesome you are, or how much you love your job or the people in your life, is truly amazing. We're merely reinforcing and reprogramming our subconscious thoughts. Remember to use words like *"I am."* Keep it in the present tense and be definite and specific. The one I use every day is, *"I am worthy of my job, the money I make, and the love of my family."*

Get in Tune With Your Body

The practice of getting in tune with your body teaches you how to scan, perceive, and attend to the subtle physical messages you receive. The body is continually sending messages about your health, emotions, thoughts, and well-being. This is a great sensory technique to improve your relationship with your body.

It seems like we spend countless hours walking, sitting, exercising, and sleeping. Do we ever get a chance to relax and examine ourselves with a so-called *"mental check-in"*? Our bodies are responding and telling us things all the time, from hunger to aches and pains.

I check in with my body during meditation, starting from my head and working down to my toes. This is a great way to scan and sense how you're feeling. I leaned on this a lot when I had surgery to repair my torn triceps. Every time I mentally scanned past my arm, I would picture my triceps healing and repairing itself. It's incredible what the mind can do.

There is research that points to the healing effects of meditation and the power to heal the body. *"With monumental health implications, meditation has been proven to naturally boost many of your body's chemicals: GABA, Endorphins, Serotonin, & more, while lowering the stress hormone cortisol. The benefits are staggering." Ref 17*

Feel the Environment Around You

Once you've been practicing meditation for a week, start to incorporate the practice of being mindful of the light and senses around you. With your eyes closed, focus, and sense the light in the room. Is it getting brighter? You'll find that when you're in a deep state of meditation you'll start to get flashes of light or, in the morning, the feeling of the sun rising even though it's still dark out.

You may have a *"white light experience"* during your mindfulness or awareness meditation session; just embrace it as a natural part of your routine. Another day, just focus on noticing sounds. What do you hear in the room or outside? I find it very relaxing listening to a nearby train or the sound of the birds chirping outside.

Lastly, try to feel the energy in the room. The simple fact is we're all made up of energy. Energy is all around us, and all that energy is giving off a frequency that we can feel. We want to take in all that positive energy so that we can use it to find love and joy in life.

Using Guided Meditation

If you google guided meditation, you're bound to find something to interest you. Although I don't use guided meditation as much as I used to, it's a handy tool when first starting out. There are so many different and useful ones. They range from beginner to intermediate and cover a multitude of topics – everything from healing and stress reduction to deep relaxation. You can also find different lengths, depending on how much time you have to spend.

The best part is that the guides walk you through, step-by-step, what to say and do. Literally; no thinking required. Traditional meditation takes practice and work, we know this, but on the chance you are new to this or just want someone to guide you through, give it a try.

Final Thoughts

I'm now several years into my meditation practice, and I feel that I've barely scratched the surface. I'm not sure how far I'll reach or what lengths of time I will get to, but I've found so much clarity and focus during my sessions. I'm very excited to learn more about myself during my 10-minute *"mind cleanse."*

Over the next few days, start to build your own daily routine. Begin with five minutes each day. Find a location that's comfortable to you – somewhere quiet – and start your own *"spiritual muscle workout."*

I've provided a 30-Day Meditation Journey guide below to help get you started. I hope that you can find some solace in your new-found mental magic, and that it serves you for many years to come. Head over to healthmindsoul.com and download your copy.

*Meditation is about
the mind muscle
connection*

~ JS

30-Day Meditation Journey

1. I'm on day _____ of my meditation journey

2. Today I meditated for _____ minutes

3. List 3 things you accomplished during your meditation

Example: breath work, guided meditation, mantras...

A. _____

B. _____

C. _____

4. Write about your experience

_____

_____

_____

5. My quote for the day!

(Write whatever comes to mind) Your affirmation or mantra

Example: I own today. This is my day!

_____

STEP 3

Reading & Journaling

When is the best time to start reading? Should I read fiction or nonfiction? What do I need to know about journaling? Should I start now? These were all things I questioned when I was first introduced to both.

The answers are completely up to you. The fact that you're reading this book now is a great start. Read whatever brings you joy. Maybe you're into novels and stories that stir the imagination or self-help books that bring out the best in you. Your mind is a sponge that never completely saturates. Fill it with as much as you can.

As far as journaling goes, yes, start now! Putting your gratitude, goals, and dreams to paper is extremely rewarding. Not only does daily journaling make you feel good, it helps you process your feelings. Keeping a journal can help you examine your thoughts and get to know yourself better. Reading and journaling have changed my life for the better and they will do the same for you.

Reading Journey

Here's a real and embarrassing fact. Before my reading journey began, I hadn't picked up a book in years. More like 20 years to be exact. It seems crazy when I actually say it out loud. Seriously that just doesn't sound right, does it? Who doesn't pick up a book and read? Answer: way more than you'd think. According *"to Pew Research Center, roughly a quarter of American adults don't read books at all. In fact in 2018, the research group released figures suggesting that 24 percent of American adults say they have not read a book — in part or whole, in print or electronically or audibly — in the past year." Ref 18*

So what spawned my interest in reading after so many years? Well, it was actually a nudge from my wife that got me started. It was early on in our relationship when she suggested I give reading a book a try. Of course I shrugged it off and didn't say much. I figured she would forget and let it be. Well she didn't.

To my surprise, later that year on my birthday she gave me a book. It was the first book I actually owned. Tell you the truth, I was excited and scared to read it. I was now committed to this book and the pressure was on to start and finish it. It looked interesting from the outset. The book was *The Mask of Masculinity* by Lewis Howes (*Ref 50*). It seemed as though it was about being a badass and the trials and tribulations of being a man. Well, it was definitely about being a man, but with all the traits that can be counterproductive in our lives.

It had many great lessons to be learned and it pulled me right in from the get-go. There were a few chapters that really tugged on my vulnerability; it was a tough pill to swallow. It felt at times as though he was talking directly to me. Truth was, I may not have wanted to but I needed to hear it.

There were many times throughout the book that I was able to reflect on my life, good and bad. I'm not ashamed to say I cried several times throughout. Not something I would have admitted 5-10 years ago. As much as I didn't like facing reality at times, I knew I needed to be open and vulnerable if I was going to make positive strides in my life.

This was the first of many books that influenced me. They all had some positive, reinforcing message that lifted my spirits and showered my mind and senses.

There are so many amazing benefits of reading beyond just the enjoyment. Here are a few things I found that are truly beneficial.

Stimulating the Mind - Whether you are a fiction or nonfiction reader, your senses will be working on overdrive the minute you pick up a book. Thoughts start flowing, your brain trying to figure out the story's plot or how you can put your new-found book to work. As you read the words in the story, your brain starts deciphering a broad range of symbols and transforming the results into ideas.

"Studies have shown that staying mentally stimulated can slow the progress of (or possibly even prevent) Alzheimer's and Dementia, since keeping your brain active and engaged prevents it from losing power.

Just like any other muscle in the body, the brain requires exercise to keep it strong and healthy, so the phrase "use it or lose it" is particularly apt when it comes to your mind." Ref 19

Reduces Stress – We've all heard that cliché about someone saying how much they would love to snuggle up on the couch, sitting by the quaint, cozy fire, reading their favourite book. Sounds terrific, doesn't it? Well, there's a good reason why.

"It's believed that reading can reduce stress and anxiety. It doesn't matter what book you read, by losing yourself in a thoroughly engrossing book you can escape from the worries and stresses of the everyday

world and spend a while exploring the domain of the author's imagination..." Ref 20

I love that statement. The fact that you can sit and read and stop worrying about life's distractions for a small period of time is impressive. Reading gets your attention and thoughts off of whatever may have been causing you stress, letting you *"Mentally detox."*

Gaining a Wealth of Knowledge -This is so true. I've gained a wealth of knowledge in the past few years. It's mind-blowing sometimes thinking about the things I've learned. I've found that when I read, and then apply what I've learned from the book to my life, I can test out what works and what doesn't. I focus on what works and remove what doesn't. From this, I've seen excellent benefits in all parts of my life. There isn't any part of my well-being that hasn't improved.

There were some surprising facts I read about some of the greatest entrepreneurs and their reading habits: Bill Gates reads around 50 books a year; Warren Buffett reads 500 pages a day; Mark Cuban reads for three hours a day; when asked how he learned how to build rockets, Elon Musk answered, *"I read books."* (*Ref 21*) As you can see, leaders are readers. It proves the point that knowledge is power.

These are some of the greatest leaders of our time. If they can spend a few minutes of their busy day reading, I certainly can carve out time in my day to read.

Improved Memory - Creeping up into my mid-40s, I'll admit I've slipped a little when it comes to my memory. My mind might not be as sharp as it once was, but reading has definitely improved my memory.

"According to a study at the Fisher Center for Alzheimer's Research Foundation, mental stimulation like reading can help protect memory and thinking skills, especially with age. The authors of the study even suggest that reading every day can slow down late-life cognitive decline, keeping brains healthier and higher functioning for longer." Ref 22

I love hearing news like that. We put a lot of effort these days into eating right and working out to look and feel great. We forget sometimes that it's imperative to *"Exercise our Brain"* as well. Our brain is our lifeline to everything. We need our minds to be sharp and focused to execute hundreds of daily tasks. Reading helps accomplish this.

Final Reading Thoughts

I want to end on this note and tell you why I think it so important to spend even 10 minutes reading a day. Funny story: my daughter, who was seven at the time, was reading a book to me for her homework assignment. I remember when she finished the book, she gazed over at me and said: *"Daddy, what books do you read?"* She caught me off guard and I was at a loss for words. I didn't want to lie to her, so I said: *"Daddy doesn't read books."* She had this weird look on her face that I couldn't quite figure out. She replied with, *"So you don't know how to read?"* I said, *"Yes, I know how to read, and I'm good at it."* She stared straight into my eyes and said, *"Then why don't you."*

It was at that moment that I knew she was on to me. I'm not sure why I wasn't reading, to tell you the truth. Here I was asking my daughter to read and telling her the importance of it, yet I wasn't setting a very good example. Yikes! I could go on with the excuses, but I won't. It was a defining moment for me. I'm glad I had that moment with my daughter.

Journaling Journey

Is it me or has journaling exploded in the past few years? I see it on the internet, read about it in books, hear it on podcasts, and find it just about everywhere I look. In our modern society, journals are being used by a wide range of people. Artists, authors, songwriters, journalists, and personal-development coaches all enjoy the power of journaling.

Journaling is a great resource for expressing and sharing your thoughts and feelings. I personally have delved into a daily routine of writing about the things I'm most grateful for. I like to envision how my day has gone or what it would look like. I even write about my dreams and desires.

Once you've put that *"Magical Ink"* to paper, you start the process of imprinting your thoughts. Those thoughts then become a form of reality. If you begin to write down your tasks, goals, and dreams, you are more likely to follow through. If you tell your mind it's true, it can't discern whether it is or isn't.

Just like reading, journaling has many benefits. I wasn't aware of any of this when I started journaling several years ago. I was in a dark place where I would have tried anything to feel better. I'm into another year of journaling and can genuinely attest to all the following attributes:

Feeling Grateful - The gratitude journal. This is my favourite thing to do when starting my day. I like to record in my journal where I want to be this week, this year, and what I see 5-10 years from now. As I go along the timeline, I'm able to assess how I'm doing and whether I've made a difference in getting where I need to go.

I like to list 5 things I'm grateful for. You can keep the list as straightforward or as detailed as you wish. It's entirely up to you. My wife and I both set aside some time each morning to make our list and share our thoughts.

In no specific order, write whatever pops into your mind. I've found that once you've printed it on paper, you're able to visualize what that gratitude looks like. Writing down what you are grateful for should be a reminder of how lucky you are. No matter who we are or how bad life might seem, we all have something to be thankful for.

Helps the Healing Process - Writing down my thoughts in my daily journal has, without a doubt, helped me with the mental healing process.

When I went through my last divorce, I had so many feelings that were difficult to process at times. Talking about my thoughts and feelings to my family and friends helped at times, but I also knew I needed an outlet where I could express my feelings with no restrictions. Sadness, happiness, and feelings of self-worth: these were all things I focused on when writing. Once I was able to write it down, it was like I just had a private counselling session. Something had been lifted off my chest.

Give it a try, I know you won't regret it.

Boost Memory - Boosting memory, you say? Who doesn't want that?

"Journaling helps keep your brain in tip-top shape. Not only does it boost memory and comprehension, but it also increases working memory capacity, which may reflect improved cognitive processing." Ref 23

I've found that when I write down my daily or weekly thoughts, I'm able to recall in more detail the events that happened during that time. Anything I can do to keep my memory in prime shape is a plus for me.

Reduce Stress and Anxiety - Journaling is a fantastic way to help reduce stress and to relax. Seriously, after writing daily about your gratitude and feelings, it would be pretty hard to feel stressed. Having that outlet to express your emotions feels great, even if the day wasn't the greatest.

We all have those not-so-great days. Even with those feelings of frustration, sadness, or anger, having a safe place to write and express those thoughts instantly relaxes and calms the body. Give it a try! You'll wonder why you didn't try it years ago.

Goals - Learning to Dream Big - I wanted to focus on this section as I believe we all need to *"Dream Big."* Believe me, I hear it all the time at home, and there are pictures of it around the house to remind me. Dreaming Big is a great way to project what you see yourself doing in the future. When you picture your future, do you have a fancy new home? Are you in that fantastic relationship you've always dreamed of?

Most importantly, write the Big Dreams down in your journal. It's best to write dreams as if they've already happened. Be specific and write in the present... I have, I am, I only, I drive, I build, I sell, I give.

This is an opportunity to *"Train Your Brain"* to believe these dreams are true.

I feel like it's easy these days to underestimate your dreams. My wife would point out that I'm more of the *"Dream medium"* kind of guy anytime I drifted off course. That might have been true years ago. Nowadays, I don't let anything block me from dreaming big. How's a million dollars sound, or the cottage in the country? These are the things I'm setting my mind and attitude to project. If we continue to set our sights low, guess what? We end up low. Set those dreams high. Shoot for the stars.

Final Thoughts

I can tell you now that I wouldn't be where I am in my reading or journaling if it wasn't for my wife. I'm thankful she nudged me in the right direction. I've read 20 plus books in the past two years. It's a crazy addiction. I only wish I had started it sooner. I'm truly *"hooked on the book."*

As for journaling, it's become a daily ritual that reminds me of all the great things in my life. I love it. I have several different journals: some for gratitude, others for free writing. But it's been a game-changer for sure.

Journaling has benefited both Tara and me so much that we collaborated on creating a journal. It's a fantastic guided journal that helps set your goals high and your dreams big. We think you'll love it. Check it out at healthmindsoul.com.

I want to challenge you to keep expanding your mind. I've included a checklist that will help get you started finding your own passion for reading. Head over to healthmindsoul.com and download your copy. If you're already off and running and reading is part of your daily routine, I'm going to challenge you to step outside your reading box and try something new. I want you to find a subject that you have been interested in but haven't had the time to read. Maybe you're wanting to learn more about spiritual enlightenment, gratitude, or healthy approaches to daily cooking. Step outside your comfort zone. You never know where it might lead.

One of my goals in writing this book was to be a springboard for you, the readers, to find out more in-depth about the subjects throughout. I've learned so much from seeing little snippets here and there in the books I read, which then led me to exploring more. Hopefully I can do the same for you. Expand your mind. Happy reading!

*Reading sharpens
the mind. Journaling
sharpens the soul*

~ JS

Joy of Reading

1. List 3 books you would be interested in reading over the next 6 months

   A. _____

   B. _____

   C. _____

2. List 3 things about those books that get you excited about reading

Ex: you love sports or novels that have been made into movies.

   A. _____

   B. _____

   C. _____

3. How will you set aside time for your reading?

   _____

   _____

   _____

4. Come up with ideas that will hold you accountable. Ex: tell your family or announce it on social media. #healthmindsoullife is a great place to start.

   _____

   _____

STEP 4

Relationships

Great relationships don't always happen immediately. They take time, commitment, sacrifice, and forgiveness. Every relationship has its ebbs and flows. Successful couples have learned how to manage the ups and downs and keep their love life strong. They learn how to work through the crazy issues of everyday life.

I know I've had my share of messy relationships over the years and as painful and heart wrenching as they were, they made me into a better father, and husband. Out of the dark, a new light has shown me things I could only have dreamed of. Luckily for me I've turned things around with the help of books, journaling, reading, writing and meditation. A strong family foundation definitely helped me through the rough times.

As I've soul searched over the past 20 years, I've finally found what I want and I'm willing to do what it takes to maintain a healthy and loving relationship.

"Always be dating." These three words have become somewhat of a staple in our household. I surely can't take credit for them. My wife said these to me during our early dating life. Here it is several years later, and we date today just like we did when we met. I'm so grateful that she shared this with me. It's a simple and easy phrase to live by, but at times can be extremely challenging. Had I known and understood that statement years earlier, I might have had insight into what it takes to maintain a healthy relationship.

I'll be the first to say my relationships, dating life, and marriages have been rocky at best. I can admit this now. Albeit, I feel ashamed and embarrassed at times. I had a tumultuous set of marriages, both quite different from the other, which ended in divorce. I wouldn't wish it on anybody, but I am who I am because of it. For better or for worse.

I had quite a different picture in my mind growing up as to how my future self would pan out. I knew I wanted to get married and have children from an early age. I wanted to be like my parents and grandparents. I admired the fact that both had long-lasting loving marriages.

In fact I distinctly remember showing up to a family reunion in my early teens. I was getting introduced to aunts and uncles I hadn't even met before. All of them had been married for decades. I'm talking 20 plus years. I thought this was going to be easy. It was practically in my blood to be in a lifetime marriage.

Marriage 1

Fast forward a few years. I joined the military and moved away at the age of 18. In my so-called wisdom I must have thought I had all the answers. Feeling like my head was on straight, life couldn't have been better. My perfect life was set in motion, just as planned...until it wasn't.

I married young and had my first daughter at the age of 22. I'll admit it was extremely tough at times. Being a Navy sailor, I put on my best face and trekked through the good and bad. By 26, I had my second daughter. This was it; I had hit the pinnacle of life. Married, two kids, it had to be easy from here. Right?

Unfortunately this is where the relationship started to fall apart. What had been an up-and-down marriage had finally hit rock bottom. Suddenly we began growing apart. We both wanted different things in our lives. Life in general was changing before my eyes. We both knew where the marriage was heading. Divorce!

This was extremely tough for me as I was raised in a church-going family where divorce was frowned upon. Now here I stood about to take a *"leap of faith"* that everything would be ok. I was separating from my wife, hoping and praying that my family would understand and that my kids would get through it unscathed; well... that leap of faith quickly turned into more than I ever bargained for. Life as I knew it started to unravel and I was falling faster and harder every day.

Here I was living in a new city, with new friends and colleagues as my only outlet. I lost contact with my parents and I had never felt so alone. I was slowly starting to fall into a deep depression. The hard times were just getting harder. Nothing seemed to go as planned. My ex-wife felt I wasn't worthy of having shared custody. I had no money to my name, and my job was growing tiresome. How life can turn on a dime is unbelievable. I never thought it could happen to me. I'd had life right where I'd wanted it months prior, and now it was at rock bottom.

Let this be lesson #1. No matter how hard or discouraging life gets, IT WILL eventually look up.

Marriage 2

Fast forward a few years post-divorce #1. I was in a new relationship with my girlfriend, who by the way lived in Canada. I know what you're thinking: divorced and now a long-distance relationship. Maybe I'm a glutton for punishment or just don't know any better. I look back now and call it the rebound relationship. Could it actually last?

Well, it did for about 12 years. I was married again a few years after moving to Nova Scotia. Of course the marriage got off to a rocky start. I should have seen the signs as things were difficult from the get-go. Being away from my two daughters in Texas and living in a new country weren't making it any easier on myself or the relationship. The one thing I did enjoy was my job; it was the one constant in my life.

Once my third daughter arrived, she became my life and soul. She had my heart from day one. My wife was travelling a lot for work and it left me with tons of one-on-one time with my daughter. It felt great. I'm sure there were moments where I was trying to overcompensate for not seeing my other daughters, but I knew I had to give her all the love I could.

Unfortunately for me, what I forgot to do was focus on marriage #2. I neglected the one thing that I thought I wanted more than anything: a happy, healthy marriage. On the home front, life was starting to get unravelled. Neither of us put the time and effort into making it a thriving marriage. It was all but disappearing once again.

At this point I was so determined to make the marriage work that I was willing to sacrifice my happiness for the sake of staying married. I knew things weren't going to get better. It didn't matter what conversations were had; this marriage was toast. I was going to have to look deep into my soul and figure out what I wanted in life and how to make it happen.

I fell into the same trap the second time around, doing the exact same things that ended the first marriage. As you can imagine we finally separated. I'm grateful that the separation was amicable, and my ex and I still get along.

Things Have to Change! - To say I've had a charmed life wouldn't be accurate. But I am blessed and grateful for the experiences that changed me to the person I am now. It would be easy to look back and talk about all the rotten things that happened. But some amazing things did happen and some beautiful girls were brought into this world.

This time around I knew I had to dissect every aspect of my failed marriages and figure out what worked and what didn't. I did not want to repeat failure again. I was on a mission of happiness. Nothing was going to stop me. I came up with my *"Relationship matrix"* of what has either sabotaged or helped me thrive.

I know I'm the last one to claim myself a relationship coach. But I've been there and done that twice. I know what has and hasn't worked and what it takes to be better. The key is the ability to learn from those mistakes and put them to work in your relationship or marriage. I believe we have all the power within us to do it.

Here are four parts of the matrix that have helped me become my better self.

The Relationship Matrix – ABD - Always be dating. I live by these words. Try to remember how exciting it was when you first met your spouse or partner. The butterflies in your stomach; the thought of seeing them filling you with joy. There's no reason you can't keep dating like that after marriage.

Date nights help bring about new experiences in relationships that have fallen into the same stale ruts that we gravitate to as creatures of habit. If you find yourself stuck in the same routine every day, a date night can be something you will look forward to all week. If you plan a creative date, you will also create fun memories together that you can cherish later on. Either way, date nights will make your future, and your past, better.

I think we all love the idea of date night. What tends to happen are the many excuses as to why we can't. We tell ourselves we have kids to watch, we're too busy at work, or we're just too tired.

Listen, I've been in that situation. I've made all the excuses. Guess what? It got me nowhere close to where I wanted to be. You have to put in the work. It's imperative. I make it a priority every month to check my calendar, and schedule a date night out.

Do whatever's in your budget. Go out for dinner, take a walk on the beach, or plan a picnic. It's too easy to get caught up in our crazy lives and forget what's really important. Get back to doing those things you enjoyed during your *"dating years."*

The Relationship Matrix – Communication - I wouldn't in a million years have thought I would be preaching how important it is to communicate with your partner. In years prior, you would have had to lock me up and interrogate me before I would talk about my feelings. I was closed up and certainly wasn't going to be vulnerable. No way!

Let's just say it was a lesson learned. You can't have a thriving relationship without communication. I have since learned to open up and express my feelings. It was not something I grew up with. It's extremely hard at times and a constant work in process.

One thing Tara and I have done to help with this is to do a weekly check-in. We talk daily, but it usually revolves around the kids or our day. Once a week, we talk about how we feel, what went well, and what didn't. I find if you can catch those little things early, they don't carry over to the point where someone blows a gasket. That never turns out good.

The Relationship Matrix - Sex - Ok, let's do the sex talk here. We need to break this down into two parts: the chemical response and the emotional impact it has on us. I mean seriously. It's a massive component of a healthy relationship. I am not even sure I have to explain why being intimate with your partner is essential, but I will. Let's first start with scientific reasons:

"Oxytocin is called "the love hormone" because it's responsible for so many of the things that make you feel good. It's crucial for social bonding of all types (romantic, platonic, familial), sexual reproduction, and birth." Ref 24

Yes, having sex releases oxytocin and a myriad of feelings that come with it. It's amazing, the fact that being intimate with your partner helps grow that bond through the chemicals released in your body. Win-win right? So now we get a glimpse from a scientific point of view. This is just part 1 of the benefits.

Part 2, for me, and the most rewarding, comes from the mental aspect of having sex with your partner. The affection, touching, kissing, and constant eye gazing has been a massive part of my relationship and the most rewarding.

I've found that once you have that deep affection with your partner, you start to build another level of intimacy, even beyond the physical touch. I believe it's something that will ignite a passion that is everlasting.

Give it a try, find those affection points with your partner. Maybe it's a gentle massage or a candlelit dinner and a glass of wine. Enjoy the process of finding what truly creates that passionate spark!

The Relationship Matrix - Forgiveness and Trust - Where do you go without either of these? Not very far, that's for sure. You can kiss your shiny relationship goodbye if trust is lost. Maybe you're one to hold grudges and not forgive. Again, I refer to communication as the answer. Letting things fester and allowing your mind to wander only leads to a lack of trust that isn't deserved. We must trust our partners to have the communication necessary for an open, honest conversation. You must learn to forgive those crazy times when you and your partner make mistakes.

Personally, when these mistakes happen to me, I don't like it one bit. I usually take a deep breath, focus my thoughts, and find the best way to deal with it. We need to be able to talk openly without judgment. Be prepared to eat crow from time to time. It's a tough pill to swallow but necessary. There's no winner or loser. It's about the end result, and that's simply to forgive. When the dust settles, you will feel lighter and free.

Have those talks, communicate, and you'll see the trust factor rise. Remember this is the person we're committed to 100%. We must trust and forgive the ones we love.

Final Thoughts

After two failed marriages, I thought I was doomed to relationships that would never succeed. It was a hard thing to swallow. I believe that the real work resides in understanding that your soulmate – or *"another half"* – exists.

We've all been through the turmoil of relationships that may not have ended well. But it's easy to believe that someone can bring you the love and joy you deserve. If you're able to acknowledge that there is a perfect someone out there for you, the universe will reflect your thoughts and desires. It may take time and heartache in between. I believe you never receive anything you don't deserve.

I've learned so much over the last 20 plus years – been through a lot of ups and downs. I wanted to relay the things I found essential in a healthy relationship. I can tell you firsthand I didn't know or follow these practices in my marriages, and I paid the price. Any relationship is going to take work. You can't just stop and leave it on cruise control. You need to stay one step ahead. Be thinking about what you can do for your partner that will let them know you're thinking of them. Don't forget to *"Always be dating."*

Lastly, I wanted to mention a book that I read that was highly beneficial in my relationship. If you haven't had a chance to read *The 5 Love Languages* by Gary Chapman (*Ref 25*), I suggest that you put this on your list of books to read. It breaks down five areas in a healthy relationship. You and your partner will get to answer a series of questions at the end of the book and find out which are your top love languages. My wife and I both had quality of time and physical touch as our top two.

Even if your languages don't match, it's a perfect tool to gauge what is important to each of you.

I've included a relationship check-in resource to help you gauge where you are and where you want to be in your relationship. I'm continually reworking my list and figuring out what works best and what doesn't. It may take some effort in the beginning, but I can tell you it's worth it in the end. Head over to healthmindsoul.com and download your copy.

Always be dating

~Tara Clements

Relationship Check-in

1. What do you love most about your partner?

   A. _____
   B. _____
   C. _____

2. What changes would you make to improve your relationship?

   A. _____
   B. _____
   C. _____

3. List something special you want to plan for your partner.

Ex: date, movie night, dinner.

_____

_____

_____

4. Plan a weekly check-in with your partner. Talk to each other about how the week went. Are there things you would change? What could have gone better? Remember, it's not the time to argue or fight about what went wrong; you're creating a safe place to talk. Checking in regularly with your partner is just one principle I recommend following for a happy, successful relationship.

STEP 5

Law of Attraction

Out of all the steps I tell you about in the book, this one had the most profound impact and was very instrumental to my mental and spiritual well-being. I have been able to apply the Law of Attraction to all areas of my life – a real *"game-changer"* so to speak. I didn't learn about the Law of Attraction until I was in my 40s.

I first heard of the Law of Attraction in early 2018. I wasn't quite sure what to make of it, but my curiosity got the best of me. I couldn't shake the feeling that I could gain infinite abundance in all areas of my life by merely having positive thoughts. It seemed so simple yet so farfetched, but I knew it was worth exploring.

After getting excited about this new-found information, I decided I would mention something to my wife. She looked at me with a smile on her face and said, "I have a book for you called the *The Secret*; you're going to love it."

I spent the next month immersed in the book. I was learning new techniques and gaining valuable insight that I didn't even know existed. To think that this knowledge has been around for thousands of years is pretty amazing. It began to feel like I had learned something that was out of this world.

I'm so excited to share what I've learned and what you can expect when you begin your journey. I'm not an expert on this subject by any means, and I'm still trying to understand the role that my mind can play in my life.

What I am now is a believer. I've personally experienced the amazing benefits of the Law of Attraction. It has manifested specific amounts of money and helped my health and career, as well as opened my mind to what was indeed possible. I know that it was the Law of Attraction (even though I didn't know about it yet) that helped me attract the perfect wife after two failed marriages. I met new people that inspired me and were instrumental in getting me where I am today.

Similar to the chapter on Meditation, I wanted to keep this chapter informative but straightforward. There are endless resources out there regarding this subject. Once you've gained experience and started putting these practices in place, I challenge you to read more about the Law of Attraction. The books by Rhonda Byrnes, *The Secret* and *The Power,* are what ignited my passion for learning more about what's possible.

Law of Attraction Essentials - Law of Attraction: what is it? And what can it do for you? I'm going to help you answer a few of these questions and touch on a few areas that I thought were instrumental in helping me find my inner peace.

The first thing we must do is break down the basic understanding of the Law of Attraction and what it is. The Law of Attraction states, *"You will attract into your life–whether wanted or unwanted–whatever you give your energy, focus, and attention to....by giving you more of whatever you are vibrating. It doesn't care whether it is good for you or not; it simply responds to your vibration." Ref 47.* That's it in a nutshell all stripped down. I love that I have control of things I put out to the universe regardless of what's going on in my life. It's our ultimate goal to be on a high positive frequency.

We must start with the basic fact that we are all made up of energy, and not just molecules and matter. Your car, your home, your coffee mug are all made up of energy. Pretty crazy, right.

"Quantum physics says that as you go deeper and deeper into the workings of the atom, you see that there is nothing there – just energy waves. It says an atom is actually an invisible force field, a kind of miniature tornado, which emits waves of electrical energy. Those energy waves can be measured and their effects seen, but they are not a material reality, they have no substance because they are... well, just electricity. So science now embraces the idea that the universe is made of energy." Ref 26

Wow, that's a lot to take in. I promise I won't bore you with too much scientific talk. I felt the exact same way when I first heard and read all these facts. I wanted you to get a basic understanding and perspective on the scientific side of things before we got into how the Law of Attraction can specifically change your life.

Money

The Law of Attraction can be immensely profound when it comes to money and wealth. There is nothing you can't manifest; there are no limitations and there is infinite abundance. Seriously, no boundaries and endless abundance. Wealth could be knocking at your door. You just have to ask. Don't we all deserve to have a share of the pie?

My personal experience with wealth and the Law of Attraction started with a meditation session where I asked for unexpected money. I admit, as much as I wanted the money, I was still having a hard time believing it could happen. I mean, how could unexpected money just show up? I wasn't getting a pay raise or a tax return any time soon. This is where it started to get fun.

I finished a meditation session where I asked the universe to keep me secure in my belief that unexpected money would show up. One week passed, then two, then three. I wanted to give up. I wanted to stop believing, but I knew I needed to stay the course and see where it would take me.

It was almost a month later when I was walking to my car that I looked to the ground and found a toonie (yes, that's Canadian for two dollars). It was only two dollars but it felt like a hundred. Somehow, someway the universe had listened and was sending me a message. The next week I found five dollars and 20 the following week. It was crazy. I certainly had never found that much money lying around before.

Later that same week, I had over 200 dollars deposited into my account. I didn't know who it was from or why. It felt like everything was coming together. The next week at work, I was called in for overtime three times. That's right! Extra unexpected money. Overtime, for me, is rare. So this was a bonus. I had over a thousand dollars come to me in just over a month. I don't believe I'm anything special. I just put my faith in the universe and it delivered when the time was right.

Money can appear in many ways; we just have to believe it has already happened. Here are a few things I found helpful in staying true to my beliefs on manifesting wealth.

"We like things to manifest right away, and they may not. Many times, we're just planting a seed, and we don't know exactly how it is going to come to fruition. It's hard for us to realize that what we see in front of us might not be the end of the story." – Sharon Salzberg Ref 27

We Must Want It to Happen - First off, we must believe that it has already happened. It's nice to wish for things but wishing leaves room for doubt. Expecting doesn't.

If we want to manifest money into our lives, we must expect it. The Law of Attraction is derived from the expectation of a specific outcome. It centres on the positive and negative energy that we conjure up in our minds. When you expect bad things to happen, they often happen. When you expect good, that often occurs as well.

There is a way to precisely manifest any amount of money into your life over time using the Law of Attraction. You must not waver from your expectation of that outcome. As long as you don't get dismayed and give up on the result, it will eventually come to fruition.

Things may take longer than expected. No worries, it will happen when the time is right. That's the universe at work. As long as we believe it in our minds to be accurate and never lose sight, it will always come to light.

You Must Act the Part - Another way that you can manifest wealth into your life is by using the Law of Attraction and acting the part. The clearer you can see the vision, the better chance you see things through. Most times, we can't envision miracles happening because we don't want to set ourselves up for failure. If we set the bar low, we shut off the ability to achieve our dreams.

While planning can help with your future, you must be able to see it in your mind as if it already happened. You must stay the course. Test drive the car you've always wanted, look at homes you envision living in. The clearer you paint the picture, the more likely you will succeed.

Health

The Law of Attraction can work miracles when it comes to your health. Having started my career in the military as a hospital corpsman, my evidence base for all healing revolved around western medicine. If you are sick, go to the doctor and get fixed. Black and White.

Yes! You should go to the doctor if you are not feeling well, but I had never really thought about using my mind as another resource to help heal. It's quite a fascinating concept:

"When a person has consistent negative thoughts their body will be further affected with the progressing manifestation of disease. When you have happy and positive thoughts, disease cannot thrive as well in your body and you will experience greater health and beauty.

Stress, anxiety, and fearful thoughts break down the body's natural immune system and causes disease to more thoroughly manifest in the body. Have you ever noticed that people who live in fear of attracting diseases are the people who typically manifest them?" Ref 28

It's incredible what the power of the mind can do. I couldn't have believed it if I hadn't experienced it myself. I recently had this theory put to the test with an injury I sustained during a workout.

It was the last week of a five-week workout challenge. The first four workouts had gone just as I had imagined, and I was feeling great. It was this last workout that scared me. I knew I could do the exercises as described, but one movement, in particular, had me scared outright. I was stressed about it all week, wondering if I should do it or not. I struggled with constant feelings of wondering if I would get hurt or wondering whether I should do the workout at all.

Well, I did the workout, and it started great. I was flying through at an outstanding pace. Finally the last movement came and that's when it came to a crashing halt. As I jumped onto the rings, I instantly heard a tear in my right triceps. I dropped to the ground clenching my arm in pain, thinking yep, I knew that was going to happen. It wasn't long after that I realized I had visualized something terrible happening to my arm just days before the competition. It was as if the universe was listening. I had sent out messages of fear and self-doubt only to sabotage myself.

Soon after the injury, I had surgery to repair the torn triceps tendon: an operation that could take many months to heal and recover. I knew at that moment I was going to have to turn my thoughts around and use them to heal my body for good. I spent countless hours during meditation and journaling expressing my gratitude toward my healed arm and positive thoughts about my body repairing itself.

Two months later I was back in the gym training. Only a month before that I couldn't even bend my arm. I think about it all the time, how powerful the mind can be when you let the positive thoughts influence how you feel. I practice and journal every day how grateful I am to be alive and healthy.

Career

I've personally put the Law of Attraction to use in my career many times. I've always had that mindset and attitude for every job opportunity that I've had. I knew when I left any interview that job would be mine. I have landed every job I've applied for and I'm incredibly grateful for every one of them.

I'm not saying it's going to be easy. It's not. You may have to go out on a limb and risk putting yourself out to the universe and let the chips fall where they may. Your attitude and mindset must be connected. Stay focused on the opportunity as if you've already been given the job!

I remember thinking about how I left California after the military to pursue a job opportunity in Texas with no guarantees, no current employment, and no place to live. I picked up and sought a new life for my family with the mindset that I already had the job. I drove over a thousand miles with my personal belongings ready to settle down in a new state with a new career and a home I didn't even have. I never would've thought I could do something so brash and reckless. I usually took the safe route, but my mind was so focused on getting the job that I knew it would all work out.

Thankfully it did. I crushed the interview and was given the job that day. It wasn't until the following week that I thought, *"Oh, Crap."* What if I hadn't gotten the job? The mindset is crucial. We must act and believe as though the outcome has already happened.

You might be thinking, that's all fine but it couldn't happen to me. Fair enough. I'm sure I would have the same skepticism. Well, it happened again, and if travelling a thousand miles for a new job wasn't far enough, try dropping everything and heading to Nova Scotia, Canada. That's right! Over 2500 miles. Yikes! I guess I'm a glutton for punishment. I felt like I was playing *"Career roulette,"* just hoping I would land on red. Well, I landed on red and secured a dream job at the children's hospital in Halifax, Nova Scotia. I have been working at the hospital for over 14 years and have loved every minute of it.

Your perfect career story doesn't have to be as dramatic as mine. What's important is that you can imagine and make your dreams a reality.

Here is a way to start visualizing your perfect career: start by finding a quiet place where you can concentrate, close your eyes, and focus on slowing down your breathing. When your body starts to relax, begin creating a mental picture of what your dream job would look like. Imagine what the place and people are like, how your friends and family will react to the news, and the excitement associated with your new career possibilities. Practice this mindfulness exercise once a day for 10 minutes.

As a final note, no matter what career you work in, attaining your dream job is probably going to require a commitment to networking with people. They can provide you with excellent references and promising leads. When you're networking, remember the Law of Attraction states *"likes will attract likes."*

Relationships

Just like money, health, and careers, the Law of Attraction can help manifest amazing relationships.

When you use the Law of Attraction to fulfill your visions of what you want in a partner, you need to match your vibrations with the frequency that you wish to receive. If you want your partner to be kind and romantic, guess what? You need to be loving and passionate.

My wife and I try to make it a habit of matching each other's frequency. We are always working on keeping our vibrations close together. The more you practice, the easier it is to know when that frequency is off. It's almost like an internal alarm sounding. It lets you know things are heading in the wrong direction. She can instantly tell the minute I'm off, and she's usually right.

Here are a few things I found imperative to applying the Law of Attraction to any relationship.

Be Open to Possibilities - You must be open to possibilities when you least expect them. They will present themselves in any fashion. I remember when I decided to get back into the dating game. I didn't think I was particularly ready as I was busy with work, coaching, and taking care of my daughter.

One day a co-worker mentioned trying a dating app. Since I was recently removed from my second marriage and had no sense of what the online dating experience might bring, I politely thanked her for the help but decided I would wait.

Over the next few weeks, she stayed persistent that online dating was the way to go. I finally caved and decided I would give it a try. It was about a month later that I had a match with my now wife. We hit it off from the start, and we haven't looked back since. What started as something of a risk – putting myself out there – turned into a beautiful relationship. Keep your eyes and mind open as you never know what might present itself when you least expect it.

Visualize the Relationship - What do they look like, what kind of job do they have, or what clothes do they wear? Whether you are in a relationship or currently looking for one, these are essential components to finding that perfect soulmate.

You must also see clearly and visualize yourself in a happy relationship. As a result, you'll walk around with the same *"loving awesomeness"* as someone who is in a happy, thriving relationship. This positive energy will then help you to attract an abundance of love and happiness like no other.

Be Grateful for Our Relationships - We must be thankful for the people in our lives if we're to have happiness and joy. We must appreciate our friends, family and, most importantly, ourselves if we expect the same from another.

It can be difficult in our social circles as we're hardwired to complain about what is wrong with our lives. Often, we don't even realize that there are solutions that exist for our relationship problems, and we end up accepting them as a fact of life.

I'm here to tell you that solitude or despair are not facts of life. Whether you are alone or not, you can be grateful for the people you do have. What people in your life are important to you? Family? Friends? Spouse?

Final Thoughts

These are just a few ways the Law of Attraction can bring infinite possibilities into your life. A quick way to know if you are on the right path and the Law of Attraction is working for you is, first, think of any object – seriously, the first thing that comes to mind. Then, picture finding or seeing this object. Keep thinking about this object and wait for it to appear. Again, it may not happen overnight or even for a while, but don't lose faith.

For me it was a pen. I described the pen clearly in my mind: what it looked like and where I might find it. I was walking to my car after work one afternoon, gazing at the sky, when something on the ground caught my eye. To my amazement, it was the exact pen I had manifested in my mind. It was a sign from the universe that I was on the right track. I had accurately pictured a black BIC pen with the cap missing, and there it was right in front of me. I scooped it up, put it in my pocket, and took it with me. I still have it in my car as a reminder that the universe is working for me.

Remember that by transforming your thoughts to focus on what you want, rather than on what you have, you can view the world in a whole new way and use the Law of Attraction to improve your life.

I've included a weekly manifestation journal to help guide you through the process. Have fun with it and remember to "*Dream Big*." Head over to healthmindsoul. com and download your copy.

What you put out to the universe will be reflected back. You better like what you see in the mirror

~ JS

Law of Attraction: Manifestation Journal

I want to provide you with a weekly manifestation journal where each day reflects either your work, wealth, health, relationships, or gratitude. It's a great way to visualize different areas of your life actively.

Monday -

Be thankful for all the money you make. Visualize where and how you'll spend your money. We must be grateful for what we have if we want to achieve more!

Tuesday -

Be thankful for the relationships you have: friends, family, loved ones. Reach out to somebody you haven't spoken to in a while or say hi to a stranger. Watch how your mood instantly improves.

Wednesday -

Be thankful for your health. Even if you don't feel well. Visualize your perfect health and what it feels like when you achieve it.

Thursday -

Be grateful for your career. Maybe you're in between jobs; that's ok. Visualize landing that new job or getting a promotion. Whatever it is, feel as though you've already accomplished it.

Friday -

Be grateful and blessed for the things in your life. Take a walk outside and visualize what your life will look like and how amazing it will be. Think of five items and give *"Thanks"* after each one.

STEP 6

Healthy Living

I was beyond ecstatic when the thought of this subject came up. I'm so passionate about living a healthy lifestyle that I wanted to share with you my experiences. I hope to pass along as much information as possible so you can start your own healthy living journey. After all, it's such a fundamental part of our lives.

I personally didn't put too much emphasis on nutrition until my 30s. That's when the importance it had on my body became apparent.

For me, my big revelation came in the summer of 2013. I was on vacation and looking in the mirror, not liking what i was seeing. It was the first time I'd been over 200 pounds. It was like it had happened overnight. I remember thinking, *"how did I gain this weight?"* I knew and I was in denial. Poor eating habits over the years had slowly crept up. One thing I've learned is you can't outwork a bad diet.

I spent the next year relentlessly working out, getting proper sleep, using recovery methods on my body, and eating a well-balanced diet. This allowed me to lose 20 pounds and keep it off for good.

As I aged, I realized I couldn't rely on my genetics or metabolism to fix everything. For me, it was always been about wanting to feel good, mentally, and physically. I wanted to be focused and have my body feel the best it could. To make that happen, I needed the proper tools under my belt.

Throughout this chapter we're going to explore four main areas I feel are necessary and essential in maintaining your overall wellness. These consist of nutrition, exercise, recovery, and sleep.

Over the years I've worked on each area separately. It wasn't until my late 30s that I was able to put all four areas in motion to complete the *"wellness cycle."* This truly is where the real magic happens. Sure, when we're young we may get away with a few less hours of sleep, a week away from the gym, or a night of bingeing on pizza and beer. But if you're anything like me, these things catch up to you fast. Sure, these things are ok if kept to short durations, but if left unattended they tend to sabotage the hard work you've already put in.

Yes, I have a nutrition plan that works for me, sleep habits, an exercise routine, and recovery methods. It's taking me years to figure out what works best. Each of us is unique and what works with one person might not work for another.

What I won't do is advocate what diet, workout program, recovery method, or sleeping habits are the best for YOU.

My goal is to bring you the fundamental information on nutrition, exercise, recovery, and sleep in the hope that it might make a difference in your life. After all, knowledge is the key to power.

Nutrition

Nutrition is as essential to our health as gasoline is to a car. We need the proper food to fuel and nourish our body, physically and mentally. It's that important! If there's anything you take away from this chapter, nutrition should be on top of the list.

As much as I love to talk about nutrition, let's be honest: the information out there can be confusing and downright scary. I wonder sometimes how we're expected to filter through all of it in the hopes of somehow finding what best suits us. The key is in finding the right balance, whatever method you decide to follow.

I believe so much in healthy eating that I'm actively pursuing my Nutrition Certifications and Diploma. I want to better myself while being able to offer sound advice to others on their pursuit of a healthy lifestyle.

We have to take care of our bodies. It's absolutely essential. Having healthy eating habits can make all the difference in the world in overall mental and physical wellness. Proper nutrition has many benefits:

"Reduce the risk of some diseases, including heart disease, diabetes, stroke, some cancers, and osteoporosis

Reduce high blood pressure

Lower high cholesterol

Improve your well-being

Improve your ability to fight off illness

Improve your ability to recover from illness or injury

Increase your energy level" Ref 29

I couldn't sum it up any better. There are so many benefits of a well-balanced diet beyond just physical appearance. How we feel inside will dictate how we feel and look outside.

I personally don't have a particular preference of one diet or another. I've tried a majority of them over my lifetime. Some have worked better than others and a lot depended on how active I was and whether I just wanted to be healthy, gain muscle, or lose weight. I think it's important to discover what works and feels best for you.

I recently tried a gluten-free, vegan diet. It worked well for a while, and I felt amazing, but in the end I went back to a more balanced approach. It's not to say I won't go back. I usually try out certain foods and see how my body responds. I like to see how mentally focused I can get or how much energy I have for my workouts.

I believe each person has to decide what is right for them. Some people can thrive on a vegan diet, while others might feel better on a more traditional balanced diet. Each body reacts differently from person to person. In the end, we all want to feel good and keep our bodies healthy and vibrant. This is going to be a lifelong journey no matter how much you think you know.

Staying on Track - We all know it can be tough to start a healthy eating regimen, and we all know how easy it is to stop. If you're having trouble keeping on track, there are several ways to help stay focused with your food choices. Life happens; it's completely natural to stray away from your healthy eating habits. The important thing is staying motivated and having the tools to get yourself back on track. We all have the ability to reach our goals even with a minor detour.

First would be to have someone hold you accountable, whether that's a spouse, family member, or nutrition coach. Let them help you stay the course. We're all going to falter from time to time, but having that person around that is *"cheering you on"* can make all the difference. It helped me immensely in my journey.

Secondly, I think it's a great idea when first getting started to keep track of all your food choices using smartphone applications that can track your daily macronutrients. Having the ability to track your water intake and food gives you a sense of control. Once you understand your portion sizes, you're well on your way.

Meal prep is a big one as well. I prep all my lunch and dinner items for the week on Sunday. It takes a little time and effort, but it is completely worth it. If I have the meals and snacks I need prepared ahead of time, it's a lot less likely that I will have to find an unhealthy alternative.

Next, don't feel bad treating yourself to a nice meal once a week, if you're having a social gathering and want to indulge. Get back on track the next day. Eating healthy is hard. There's no sense in making it harder by guilting yourself into feeling bad for splurging a little.

Lastly, with the explosion and ease of fast food these days, I thought it was an extremely important thing to talk about. Jumping through the drive-thru or walking into your nearest fast-food restaurant tends to happen more often than one would like to admit.

"According to the Food Institute's analysis of data from the Bureau of Labor Statistics, millennials alone spend 45 percent of their budget's food dollars on eating out." Ref 7

That's pretty astonishing. A few nights of fast food won't sabotage your healthy lifestyle. But making a habit of eating out could end up doing a number on your health. Moderation is critical; you've worked too hard to eat yourself out of good health.

The best part of nutrition is that we're in control. We determine what we put in our bodies. We have the choice each and every day to treat our bodies well.

Exercise

Exercise has always been a staple in my life. I grew up playing soccer and baseball, swam any chance I could get, and played outside as much as possible. Exercise was something I enjoyed because it was fun.

Unfortunately, somewhere in my late 20s I started to lose that youthful enjoyment. Exercise began to seem like a chore: something I had to do but didn't really want to. I needed to find that *"thing"* that would get me excited about my health and well-being again.

Luckily for me this is where weightlifting and running came into my life. Although running has come and gone, I did reach my goal of running a marathon: definitely a major highlight and proof that anybody can achieve if they believe. Weightlifting has continued to stick around, and I've been actively involved for the past 20 years.

No matter what choice you make, the key is to find something you love. We have more choices than ever when it comes to exercising. There are fitness centres popping up on every corner it seems. At-home workouts and home gyms are super trendy. Group classes are super fun too. There are so many reasons to stay active, and there's no one-size-fits-all approach.

Here are a few reasons why exercise is essential to overall health.

"Help you control your weight

Help your body manage blood sugar and insulin levels.

Improve your mental health and mood

Strengthen your bones and muscles

Improve your sleep" Ref 30

I know I've personally seen a change in all aspects of my life due to exercise. I sleep like a baby, and feel less stressed and more relaxed after working out.

If you currently exercise or want to start, I challenge you to try something new. Maybe you're interested in kayaking or karate, but not quite sure if it's for you. That's ok. Take a friend and try it together. If it's not for you then at least you have someone to share the story with.

If you still can't find anything, check with friends or social media and see what they're doing. Yes, you might be scared or hesitant. Getting out of our comfort zone once in a while can be a good thing.

I took a leap into the unknown several years ago. I was your typical gym-rat, lifting weights and running the treadmill. It's what I knew and was comfortable doing. In 2016 I ventured into my local CrossFit box. I was intimidated at first and surely had my doubts. After a few classes and meeting some really great friends, I can now say I've found something I'm truly passionate about. I've been doing it for the past four years and love it. I enjoyed it so much I ended up becoming a coach. It's the best of both worlds. I get to work out, be a coach, and help others on their exercise journey.

No matter what you choose to do, whether it's a 10-minute walk or a three-mile run, the key is to be active. When we were kids, we enjoyed doing anything as long as we were moving. There's no reason we can't do the same again.

Recovery

Recovery has played a massive part in my life as it relates to sports and exercise. It wasn't until I was in my 40s that I knew I would need to focus on taking better care of my body. There was no way I could stand the day-to-day rigours of the gym if I wasn't going to put the time in to take care of myself. After all, I want to be healthy, mobile, and as pain free as possible as I age.

We're going to touch on five recovery methods I've found highly conducive to any exercise routine. Chiropractic care, Massage, Stretching, Yoga, and Physiotherapy are five amazing supplemental routines anybody can add to their wellness routine. They have become essential in helping me to avoid injury as well as treat ongoing ailments.

Chiropractic Care - Let's first get into what it is they do and how they can help:

"A health profession concerned with the diagnosis, treatment and prevention of mechanical disorders

of the musculoskeletal system, and the effects of these disorders on the function of the nervous system and general health. There is an emphasis on manual treatments including spinal adjustment and other joint and soft-tissue manipulation." Ref 31

It's a profession that's been around for at least a hundred years, and to this day I find there's still skepticism surrounding what chiropractic care is and whether it's beneficial.

I'll admit I felt the same way the first time I went. I had tweaked my neck working out. I was referred to a chiropractor for an initial assessment. She first took some diagnostic readings that showed the tension of my muscles in my back and how it was causing a misalignment of my spine. I kind of always knew it, but this just brought it to light.

As she adjusted my back and neck I could instantly feel relief. I had several treatments over the course of a few weeks, and I felt better as the months went on. I finally reached the point at which I started to buy into what was happening to my body and how it could fix me.

The chiropractic profession and practice has skyrocketed in the last few years.

"The American Chiropractic Association estimates that there will be 80,000 chiropractors in the United States by 2020, up from 58,000 in 2010, with chiropractic colleges graduating about 3,000 new practitioners each year. A 2007 study found that more than 18 million Americans had been treated with spinal manipulation, the core of chiropractic practice, during the previous year, a number that has likely increased since then." Ref 32

I'm not advocating one way or another, just trying to inform you how it affected me. It's something that most insurance companies cover and is definitely worth trying. You'll never know unless you go.

Massage - "Massage therapy is a type of treatment in which a trained and certified medical professional manipulates the soft tissues of your body — muscle, connective tissue, tendons, ligaments and skin — using varying degrees of pressure and movement." Ref 33

I started massage therapy several years ago after constantly having aches in my back. It has been a game-changer and I haven't looked back. This one is hands down the best bang for your buck...and again most insurance companies cover it. It's a shame I let all those years go by without going.

Nowadays I schedule a massage once every 30 days. I find by the end of the month, my body starts to feel tense and tightens up. The massage puts me right back at ease. It's incredibly calming, and there are many techniques available depending on your comfort levels. I like deep tissue as it gets my muscles extremely relaxed.

If you haven't been, GO! You'll wish you went sooner.

Stretching - I'll be the first to say I was never a person who spent 10-15 minutes before a workout stretching and warming up, or even cooling down after for that matter. Luckily, in my younger years I was able to escape my workouts without injury. Warming up would undoubtedly have benefited me in the long run. Over the years, as my muscles have stiffened, I have started to realize the importance of static and active stretching.

After multiple sessions with my physiotherapist, massage therapist, and chiropractor, they all explained how my muscles were extremely tight and not allowing a proper range of motion. They also explained how this was the cause of a lot of my joint and spine issues.

It was enough to get me interested in learning to properly warm up and cool down. *"A warmup gradually revs up your cardiovascular system by raising your body temperature and increasing blood flow to your muscles. Warming up may also help reduce muscle soreness and lessen your risk of injury. Cooling down after your workout allows for a gradual recovery of preexercise heart rate and blood pressure." Ref 34*

I recently started to incorporate a warm-up routine according to my workouts and the body parts I would be working on. I've also tried to implement a cool-down routine. I'll admit I have to get better as I easily get distracted and tend to chat with my buddies more than stretching after a workout. Having said all that, I found that when I did do a cool-down routine, my soreness after workouts was less, and my muscles weren't as tight the next day.

Yoga – "Where have you been all my life?" It took me quite a while to warm up to the idea of going to a yoga class. I wasn't sure how much I would get out of it. Boy was I wrong. The first time I went to a yoga class, I remember shaking on my mat during a warrior pose. My shirt was soaked, and I had a hard time even doing the basic movements. I'm thankful the instructor was patient and encouraging. I left my session with a new-found respect.

These days I find it hard to get to a yoga class. Usually, I wait until my wife, who runs her own health and wellness business, schedules something for her clients. It makes for the perfect opportunity. If you haven't tried a class, I highly recommend you take a friend or colleague and go.

There are some amazing benefits to yoga as well:

"Increased flexibility

Increased muscle strength and tone

Improved respiration, energy and vitality

Maintaining a balanced metabolism

Weight reduction

Cardio and circulatory health

Improved athletic performance

Protection from injury" Ref 44

Besides all these great benefits, I find you can really get in tune with your body.

Physiotherapy - Ok, so we're on to our last recovery method and one of my favourites. For me it's been a key cog in my training regimen. Over the last few years, I've made seeing my physiotherapist mandatory to help me recover from sprains or strains and, as of recently, a torn triceps. Nonetheless, we all could benefit from seeing a physiotherapist when needed. Whether you're a casual walker or a weekend warrior athlete, we're all prone to injury at some point.

I will be the first to admit I wasn't as informed about physio treatments as I could have been. I knew about them through word of mouth from those that had sought out therapy. But usually the therapy was post-surgical, or for a traumatic injury. It wasn't until my fellow workout partner, who is a physiotherapist, explained what he could do for me, and how it could help me. He was able to assess, treat, and help me recover from multiple injuries. I'm thankful every day for the help he provided in my recovery process.

I asked my physiotherapist, Mike Conners, to talk about the recovery process I went through and how it can relate to others going through similar situations. It wasn't just the physical rehab but the mental support throughout that helped get me through. It took many months of intense rehab and hard work, but I know if I can get back to 100% so can you!

My Rehab Story:
Thank you Jeff for the opportunity to talk about physiotherapy, your treatment, and our journey together.

This journey began 4 years ago when Jeff and I met at our CrossFit gym. I was new to the sport and Jeff was one of the individuals who helped me through the first three months when most new CrossFit athletes look more like a deer in headlights than an athlete.

It's a typical progression into the sport where you learn new language, techniques, and skills. This is often the make-or-break period for many participants. There are many reasons why people discontinue sports or fitness routines in general during this time. Some leave due to frustration or self-doubt, others because it's more difficult and/or time consuming than they expected, and some unfortunately leave due to injury. I guess that's where I come in.

I knew right away that I loved the sport and I would continue it moving forward, but I didn't realize what an impact it would have on me and my professional path.

During the initial months I found myself fascinated with the parallels between CrossFit and physiotherapy. As a physiotherapist I spend much of my day teaching people how to move better, more safely, and more efficiently. The principles of CrossFit meld perfectly with this and I knew I wanted to take on a bigger role. So as I progressed, I found my place within the sport as an athlete, coach, and physiotherapist for other athletes.

My relationship with Jeff is unique in the physio/patient world. It began as two athletes pushing each other in class and has developed into a friendship where we are coaches, teammates, and training partners, and eventually became physiotherapist and patient – which has brought us to the point we are today.

Many people think of physiotherapy as retroactive. It's seen as a service needed once an individual is injured. This is not always the case and nor should it be. Being proactive is the key to becoming a better athlete and a stronger, healthier individual. This is a conversation that Jeff and I have had many times while working after class on skill development.

Oftentimes there is a reason someone is not advancing in a skill. These reasons can often be related to external factors outside the gym such as sleep, nutrition, hydration etc. However one of the key aspects can be found in the way we move. This is related to a person's size, shape, strength, biomechanics, and motor skills. By addressing these issues early, we have the potential to improve skill and prevent injury. This could be as simple as increasing someone's shoulder range of motion to decrease their potential for neck and shoulder pain in an overhead position, or addressing muscle imbalances in the lower extremity that often results in injury to the knees or the back. The best way to achieve this is through open dialogue between the coach, athlete, and physio.

Over the past three years I have been able to help Jeff through a few minor injuries by working on movement patterns and changing muscle recruitment patterns. We believe this has had a positive impact on his training by improving form and decreasing injury times, which allows him to train harder and safer. Proactive maintenance of the body is critical in performance.

In October, Jeff suffered a severe and fairly uncommon injury. He suffered a ruptured triceps while performing Ring Muscle Ups. This was an interesting situation for me as a physiotherapist because I was competing with Jeff at the same time, therefore I saw the injury in real time. Rarely as a physiotherapist can you say you were there when the injury occurred and followed it all the way through every day until the end.

Over the next 8 months our rehab was quite extensive. Not only did we see each other in the clinic, where we worked on the basics of healing the surgically repaired tendon through range of motion and strength, but we also worked at the gym on preparing Jeff for every phase of rehab. Sometimes it was scaling options while other times it was simply encouragement.

Injuries have a significant impact on an athlete's psychology. For this reason I believe it is critical to get an athlete back to some form of his or her sport as quickly and safely as possible. In the gym this is very easy as there are such a variety of skills within the sport, and countless scaling options that allowed Jeff to advance other skills while he was rehabbing his arm. This gave Jeff minor victories every day; it allowed him to have a smooth progression through rehab because he was never in an idle state.

As we reached each milestone, we opened up new skills that we progressed through systematically. I feel that this had as much of an impact on Jeff's mental state as it did on his physical. Though he was using one arm for the early stages, he never lost his metabolic conditioning or strength in other areas of the body. If anything he became stronger, which will ultimately make him a better and stronger athlete going forward.

Jeff was not an injured athlete, but rather one who wanted to better himself by correcting any faults or imbalances that he had. This process was more about high performance and optimization of training.

Over that time he suffered an unrelated injury which led us initially back to a traditional model of physiotherapy care during the acute stages. We were then able to take two paths moving forward by working on traditional tissue healing, strength, and range of motion while continuing to work on other faults simultaneously. Finally in the last phase we worked on higher-skill activities to lead him to a full return to sport. This final stage meant pushing his physical and mental capabilities together so that, as his strength and function improved, so did his confidence.

I am happy to say that with everything he did at home, in the clinic, and in the gym, he is well on his way to a very successful return to the sport he loves. Ref 45

Hopefully you can take away a better understanding of how physiotherapy can support your everyday fitness goals and routines no matter how big or small. At the end of the day we all want to be healthy, fit, and mentally prepared for the challenges ahead.

Sleep

I'm not sure I can advocate for something more these days than the importance of sleep and the profound effects it has on our bodies. I do believe there has been a movement in the last few years on the benefits of sleep and the effects it can have on recovery, muscle growth, fat loss, and an overall sense of well-being.

I remember those days of staying up late and getting up early, going to work, hitting the gym, and doing it all again the next day. Well, I can tell you firsthand that, being in my mid-40s, I can no longer do that. Anything less than seven hours of *"quality"* sleep, and I'm toast the next day. My energy and mental focus the next day also suffer. I would recommend no matter what age you are that you get the required sleep for *YOU*.

I believe sleep is the engine that drives nutrition, recovery, and exercise to the next level. This is the one that the other three depend on to make things magically happen. Here are a few benefits of getting quality sleep that I find essential.

"Getting enough sleep is essential for helping a person maintain optimal health and well-being. When it comes

to their health, sleep is as vital as regular exercise and eating a balanced diet.

Better productivity and concentration

Better calorie regulation

Greater athletic performance

Lower risk of heart disease" Ref 35

I think it goes without saying, we all know the importance of sleep and the effect it has on us positively and negatively.

If you believe you are getting the hours you need every night but still aren't feeling rejuvenated, try a sleep tracker. They are definitely worth the investment. Most smartwatches these days have them as well. A sleep tracker can give you an idea as to how much quality sleep you're getting each night. Now, it won't help you sleep better, but it could give you insight into your sleep habits.

I want to leave you with some great tips for improving and tracking your sleep:

1.   Keep the room as dark as possible

2.   Keep the room as cool as possible

3.   Turn off all electronics one hour before bed.

Final Thoughts

I think we have exhausted all the potential ways we can benefit from sleep, exercise, recovery, and nutrition. The key isn't to go out and attack all these areas tomorrow. That just has failure written all over it. If you feel exercise is easy for you and you have a weekly routine that sets you up for success, that's great. Maybe you need to tighten up your nutrition. So start with that first, and come up with a plan that works for *YOU*. When you feel your diet is on point, move on to something like recovery or sleep. Eventually, you will have all aspects coming together. You'll be amazed how each one feeds off the other.

It's your time to take control of your life and make the changes necessary for success. Having people in your corner that support you and understand the importance of a healthy lifestyle is crucial. We can't go at this alone.

I wanted to leave you with something to kick-start your healthy living life. I put together a checklist to help you examine all the areas of your healthy living routine. This is a great way to start each day. Check us out online. We have lots of resources and information to help you achieve the best YOU! Head over to healthmindsoul. com and download your copy.

Healthy Living Checklist

1. Drink up – try to get seven to eight glasses of water a day

2. Get your sweat on – try to squeeze in 30 minutes of exercise a day

3. Stretch it out – make time to stretch your muscles each day

4. Plan for recovery – make your appointment for massage, physio, chiropractic

5. Plan ahead – plan meals in advance to keep progress on track

6. Journal your tasks – writing down your fitness and nutrition goals will help to solidify all the hard work you've put in

7. Mindful eating – try to slow down your eating; this will help with digestion and satiety

8. Positive attitude – enjoy the process. It doesn't have to be daunting. Laugh more and surround yourself with positive people

9. Digital detox – try to shut down all phones and computers one hour before bed

10. Get quality sleep – always aim for six to eight hours of sleep a night

*Nutrition and Fitness;
a lifetime battle worth
fighting*

~ JS

STEP 7

Gratitude and Blessings

"Gratitude is a thankful appreciation for what an individual receives, whether tangible or intangible. With gratitude, people acknowledge the goodness in their lives…. As a result, gratitude also helps people connect to something larger than themselves as individuals — whether to other people, nature, or a higher power." Ref 36

I'd like you to think of something for which you feel grateful. Maybe it's your children, your significant other, the house you live in, or the career you worked so hard to get. It could be how you recovered from an illness or sickness. Maybe it's someone who's made a significant impact on your life. It could be an incredible trip you took to a foreign country, or the family gathering at Christmas.

Whatever it is that comes to you, I'm asking that you be mindful of the thoughts you have about the circumstances for which you're grateful. I want you to feel the positive mindset of gratitude. It will open and expand your mind to the highest possible vibrations.

It's not until you start to practice gratitude that you'll be able to be grateful for those defining moments in your life. Sure, when life gives you lemons it might seem like you're doomed, and it might feel like uncertainty is lurking around the corner. There are those moments in life that hit you like a brick, but they also become the opportunities to take what you've learned and improve. Don't squander them away. I've realized now that every moment, relationship, and situation is a chance to be grateful for the life you've been given.

As I've continued to work on my inner peace, four things really stood out that I thought were essential in promoting a life filled with gratitude and love: setting aside time each day to practice gratitude, finding good in everything, recognizing the healing powers of gratitude, and improving mental toughness.

We're going to take a dive into each and find out what it is we can do to keep living the life we've always wanted: a life full of love and gratitude.

Setting Aside Time Each Day to Practice Gratitude

Gratitude Journaling - "Gratitude journaling is the habit of recording and reflecting on things…that you are grateful for on a regular basis. In essence, you are rewiring your brain to focus more on the positive aspects of your life and build up resilience against negative situations. Keeping a gratitude journal is a popular practice in positive psychology - the scientific study of happiness. It's commonly also referred to as 'counting your blessings' or 'three good things.'" Ref 37

It's amazing how we can put our thoughts into words and then those words end up having such a profound impact on our psyche. I'm a huge believer that we should start our mornings with daily gratitude. It should be a foundation, a rock, a starting point for your day. I've personally been practicing gratitude through journaling for over 2 years now, and I can tell you it's a difference-maker.

There are many journal variations you can choose from, focusing on things from gratitude and daily affirmations to general mindful thoughts. I enjoy writing about all three and love the feeling of pen to paper. As far as paper journals go, the sky's the limit. I've tried out a few that I've really enjoyed. The wife and I collaborated on our own journal and are excited to see it come to fruition. If you're having a hard time finding a starting point for your gratitude journaling, go to healthmindsoul.com and check out some tips on journaling.

Whatever it is you decide to do, make a routine you're able to follow. It can be difficult to stay on course when you're dealing with life's distractions or trying to adjust to the negativity in the world. Just remind yourself to take a few minutes every morning to see the goodness in your life. You will immediately see the energy vibrations change for the day ahead.

There's something special about taking time each day to write down the things you're grateful for. Those moments then take over your conscious feelings. While you're journaling, you should avoid social media and news feeds, email, and your daily chores. Fill your mind with excitement.

It's in that moment that you feel as though something special is unfolding right in front of you. You're deciding to not let in the negativity. You're creating a positive attitude. We all know what the reality of the world is, and that's not going to change anytime soon. At least for the 10 minutes of journaling you can take control of your positive mindset.

Mindfulness Meditation – "Gratitude meditation enables you to truly be thankful for all things, the good and the bad, because it's all happened for a reason. Every experience, heartache and milestone took place to specifically shape you into the person you are; what a thing to be grateful for!" Ref 38

The practices of gratitude and meditation were absolutely meant to be a pair. As I stated in Step 2, meditation is an amazing time to practice gratitude as our minds are at an extremely high frequency. We're full of thoughts and ideas.

Gratitude meditation is the practice of mindfulness and reflection on things we're grateful for. It's about finding that genuine feeling of appreciation and love, whether it's for family, friends, a beautiful sunset, or the aroma of your favourite coffee. It can be anything you can envision as positive in your life. Maybe it's a successful recovery from an injury, or a life lesson you conquered where you came out the other side the best version of *YOU*!

It's easy these days to get caught up in current events and the negativity online, but in reality, those things rarely have an impact on us in our daily lives. A grateful meditation isn't about tuning out the events and mishaps of our society completely. It's a way to focus us back to a place of personal reflection and attitude. Take a few minutes each session to focus on gratitude.

Here are a few ideas to add to your morning meditation routine:

Once you've focused yourself on breathing and slowed your breaths, start to feel gratitude for being alive and healthy.

Perhaps you are grateful for your home, the food you eat, your career or the money you make.

Next, bring your focus to people who positively influence you in your life and how blessed you are with their presence.

Lastly, feel gratitude for yourself and your incredible life and be thankful for all that you have been blessed with.

Finding Good in Everything

Don't allow other people's bitter attitude or negativity to influence your inner peace. Look for the light in all people, and believe there's good in everyone.

Anger, failure, and judgment are a way of life; don't let them become your go-to attitude. The last thing we want to do is become reliant on these as a default mechanism. Instead, choose to live in gratitude.

There are going to be plenty of times life does not go the way you've planned. It could be your job, family, or health that end up compromised. Just remember there is always something in your life that you can be grateful for. You need to keep in mind the big picture, and the road bumps that challenge you from time to time will make you stronger. If you can get through the tough patches, it will be easier to find the things you are blessed with when they pass.

I've been down this road before, and I can tell you it will be tough. If life gets bumpy and you're feeling down or wondering when things will look up, try getting out of your comfort zone and spend time practicing gratitude in other ways.

Here are a few things I found that instantly brought me back into perspective with the goodness in life:

Being Present – I've always had a tendency to think everything through, spending countless hours looking ahead. Meanwhile, I'd be missing the current moments right in front of me. If you can learn to be present in your life at any moment with a feeling of gratitude, you will be able to handle situations that come your way, and your positive energy and excitement for life will be enhanced.

Surround Yourself with Positive People - You are who you are because of the five closest people around you; this couldn't be more accurate. There are ways to find positivity in the world, and one way is to surround yourself with loving people. If you're having trouble getting yourself out of the constant gloom and doom, then surround yourself with friends and family you can talk to that will provide that inspiration and drive. There's no better distraction when you've fallen on hard times than to be surrounded by loving, supportive people.

These days more than ever I make it a habit of surrounding myself with awesome people – people who I strive to be like. Whether it's in their personal or professional lives, they radiate positive energy, and it's contagious. It's easy to feel alive when others are doing the same.

Drop the Judgment - Nowadays, more than ever, it's easier to get caught up in the act of judgment. With the rise of social media, we are now putting ourselves out there to the world, opening ourselves up for interpretation. It goes both ways as it is easier than ever to fall prey to judging others as well, hidden deep behind the mask of the internet. I believe when you are grateful, you can't simultaneously put out negative vibrations.

I've been in situations where a person is talking negatively about someone else. It doesn't matter whether you think they're right or not, it's easy to wonder if they might be talking wrong about you behind your back. Remember, vibrations are more than just words and feelings. They are frequencies that are felt by others.

Have you ever noticed when you're around someone who is having a bad day you get the feeling something is wrong? Or when you're talking good about someone, all of a sudden, they show up? It is the power of gratitude.

Judgment can be contagious, and it's the complete opposite of what we're striving for. If we can take a few minutes to reflect on the conversations we're having with others and ask ourselves if this is improving our quality of life, we might just end up improving our overall well-being.

Recognizing the Healing Powers of Gratitude

It's pretty mind-blowing that, through the power of gratitude, we can heal our bodies and minds. Studies have shown the incredible effects it can have.

"Canadian researchers found that people who wrote letters of thanks or performed good deeds for a mere six-week period were able to improve their mental health, decrease their bodily pain, feel more energetic and accomplish more daily tasks for up to six months." Ref 39

Through my observations, I've noticed that grateful people tend to experience more joy and love for life. They tend to shy away from bitterness, judgment, and disdainful attitudes. They take the stress from everyday life and turn it into something positive. We all know how stress can wreak havoc on our bodies and minds.

Here are a few things that I found improved when I practiced my daily gratitude.

Fitness Levels Improved - When you're feeling blessed about life and health, you tend to be more inclined to hit your fitness goals. You'll want your mind and body running at its best. Have you ever had those crazy days at the job where you were stressed and overworked? The last thing you wanted to do was go to the gym or work out. When you're feeling great about life, it's easier to get motivated and keep a positive mindset, making sure you get your daily exercise.

Quality of Sleep - As someone who has never had a problem sleeping, I can tell you without a doubt that when things are off in my life, or negativity has set in, my sleep turns to crap. I toss and turn, my mind wanders, and I'm usually exhausted the next day. The effects often linger for several days.

"Grateful people sleep better. Writing in a gratitude journal improves sleep, according to a 2011 study published in Applied Psychology: Health and Well-Being. Spend just 15 minutes jotting down a few grateful sentiments before bed, and you may sleep better and longer." Ref 40

When you're falling asleep, you're more likely to think of negative and stressful situations, and less likely to think positive thoughts. It feels as though my negative vibrations impair sleep, and when I'm in gratitude, I'm relaxed and able to get that quality sleep I need.

Focused Mind - When you're in a state of gratitude, a revolving cycle starts and begins to influence how you feel about life and society. You start to rely on the positive forces in your daily routine. You begin to notice there are more positives in your life than you previously thought.

I find when I'm practicing my mindfulness, I start to notice little things that I otherwise wouldn't have seen before. Even walking down the street I notice the sounds of the birds or the swaying of the trees. Keep your phone or music off. Start to get in tune with your thoughts and nature. Take a minute the next time you're out to give thanks three times for something you're grateful for and watch how everything brightens up.

Feeling Less Anxious or Depressed - I feel better when I'm in a continual state of gratitude. No matter what's thrown at me during the day, I can spin it into something worthwhile. When you practice daily gratitude, you'll feel more energy, excitement, and longing for what's to come. You'll sleep amazing at night and be ready to take on the world every day.

So how is it that the practice of gratitude can give us such an uplifting feeling and suppress depression?

"Scientists say that these techniques shift our thinking from negative outcomes to positive ones, elicit a surge of feel good hormones like dopamine, serotonin and oxytocin, and build enduring personal connections.

The insight and reflection of counting these moments is what makes the practice of gratitude so powerful. But the key to combating depression is making these positive experiences part of the fabric of your life." Ref 41

Improving Mental Toughness

We all have the resilience and ability to promote gratitude. Rather than complaining about the things you don't have in your life that you think you deserve, ponder a few minutes to concentrate on everything you have. Start to develop a positive attitude and get your mind-muscle workout.

"Gratitude increases mental strength. For years, research has shown gratitude not only reduces stress, but it may also play a major role in overcoming trauma....A 2003 study published in the Journal of Personality and Social Psychology found that gratitude was a major contributor to resilience following the terrorist attacks on September 11. Recognizing all that you have to be thankful for— even during the worst times—fosters resilience." Ref 42

Each day is an opportunity to build your memory and build a resume filled with gratitude. Journaling, meditation, and mantras are all things that can improve your mental toughness.

Lastly, don't forget to pay attention to the negative habits that deny you the real mental workout you so need. Feeling bad about yourself or giving up on your dreams after failing are just a few things that can be a cause for concern when it comes to building your mind. Giving up those bad routines will help your mental toughness.

Final Thoughts

Remember to thank people no matter what the deed or task they provide. There is nothing too small or too minuscule to always give thanks for!

When you're used to running at a fast pace, you start to overlook the small things in your life. You forget to appreciate the things that truly matter. You should take time to reflect and appreciate a thousand things happening daily in your life. Being present can empower your current situation as you begin to focus on the essential people and circumstances that really matter.

Practicing gratitude helps you feel grounded and peaceful; it will improve your ability to share that love with others. My wife once told me, *"Do you want to be the person who lights up the room when you walk in or lights up the room when you leave"* If you practice your gratitude towards others you will be assured to light up the room when you enter.

A quick thought the next time you're feeling those negative vibrations. It is impossible to be unhappy and grateful at the same time. If you want to get out of the funk you're in, slowly work on getting back to the right place – little steps at a time. Think of something positive in your life, maybe your spouse, kids, career. Then find another and another until you've come back to your original state of happiness. I've tried this technique many times. It might feel a little unusual the first go-round, but be assured it *WILL* bring you back to a positive mindset.

As we exit this chapter, I want to leave you with a worksheet that will help you examine some life situations and moments that define the importance of gratitude in your everyday life. Head over to healthmindsoul.com and download your copy.

No matter what negativity has been thrown your way, get back up and live life to the fullest

~ JS

What Are You Grateful For?

Today is my day! I'm thankful for all that I have and all that I am.

1. List 3 people you're grateful to have in your life

Ex: a friend, family, co-worker

A. _____

B. _____

C. _____

2. List 3 things that are the most important in your life. Ex: family, career, and health

A. _____

B. _____

C. _____

3. What is something or someone you took for granted in your life? How would you have changed it?

_____

_____

4. What is something amazing that has happened to you in the past year?

_____

_____

STEP 8

Forgiveness and Joy

Forgiveness, fears, and joy are things that impact us the most mentally and physically on a daily basis. We as a society have put on so much emotional armour that we're so afraid to expose the pain and fears in our lives. We're so stubborn beyond belief that we've forgotten to forgive others – especially ourselves. If we are to be the best version possible, we have to and must forgive ourselves, period.

As I've worked on my shortcomings and deficiencies over the years, I've come to find four missing components that should have become cornerstones to a loving and forgiving life: forgiving ourselves, putting aside our emotional armour, finding our joy, and facing our fears.

I thought they were important enough to discuss in this chapter. Let's get to it!

Forgiving Ourselves

Forgiving ourselves and moving forward can be easier said than done. I believe that to forgive yourself will require absolute compassion and understanding. You have to remember that it's also a choice. Your choice!

It doesn't matter whether you're trying to reconcile a small problem or something big and drastic, the steps required to forgive yourself are going to look the same.

The age-old saying *"All of us make mistakes at times, we're humans"* couldn't be more accurate. The key is to take those lessons, learn, and move on from them. There might be some harrowing feelings, but as uncomfortable as it may be, some painful things are worth going through. Forgiving yourself is one of them. Here are a few steps that can help you face your fears.

Write Down Your Mistakes - If you make a mistake and struggle to let it go, talk it out in your head and write it down. When you put pen to paper, you've given credence to the thoughts in your head. You can then start to free yourself from the burden you carry. If I haven't already mentioned it several times, journaling is a fantastic way to get your thoughts out daily. The less internal garbage we carry around, the less chance we let it take control of our lives.

Take Each Mistake as a Learning Experience - It's imperative to take each error as a new learning experience. We use what we learned in the past, and we work on improving what we wish for in our current life.

We must remind ourselves that what we did at the time was the best we could do with what we knew. We didn't have a crystal ball or a fortune teller to predict the outcomes. We went with our gut instincts or reactions. Once we understand why we did it, we'll be better equipped to forgive ourselves and move forward.

Quit Hitting Rewind - Ever have those moments when things didn't go quite as planned, and everything went out of sorts? You were upset and angry only to replay that same moment day in and day out. Maybe you've spent many days stewing about something you didn't like. It's human nature to spend time and energy replaying and processing your mistakes. It's ok to take time and discuss your feelings. Still, dwelling on your mistakes over and over again is only going to inevitably slow the healing process and not allow you to take the steps necessary for forgiveness.

If you catch yourself playing the *"woe is me"* or *"everything happens to me"* card, it's time to stop and reflect on the situation. Take a deep breath, go outside, meditate, journal. Find something that gives you a moment to assess the outcome of your actions.

Putting Aside Our Emotional Armour

It may be challenging to face the realities of your life, and it might be that you're afraid of what's behind door number 1 or what's lurking in your past. It could be you don't know what to do, or you're fearful of getting hurt again. This is when emotional armour comes to fruition and protects us against life's cruelty.

Unfortunately, the thing that happens when you do that is you end up hiding your true self and not living up to your amazing potential. Sometimes it can be so easy that this becomes your new persona and turns you into the person you are today.

We're so afraid these days of showing people the real us. We know that we can put on the armour anytime we want to protect ourselves from the agony and pain. Unfortunately, we need this pain to make the breakthrough into being the person we are to become. I know all too well the ability to put on the emotional armour.

I grew up in a family that didn't share their feelings or express much emotion. I kept things in and was on guard at all times. It was reasonable to me that I should do this, and it wasn't something I thought too much about. When I turned 18 and joined the military this only added fuel to the fire, as it was a culture that embraced emotional armour.

Having to put on a stoic sense of being all the time was tough. No matter how I felt or what I believed, I kept my head down and moved about life without a real sense of direction. I loved my time in the military and I'm ok with how that worked, it just added to the armour I was already wearing.

I had to put on a face that wasn't mine. At least not all 100%. I wanted to be free to express and do the things I enjoyed. I'm so blessed these days to have someone in my life that loves me for me and accepts who I am, flaws and all.

Believe it or not, when you put on emotional armour, you deny yourself the opportunity to live your authentic life. It's almost as if you were building a wall in front of your journey on purpose. But the thing is, we need to see over that wall if we're to be our true selves. With that barrier, you'll never open up to yourself, others, and the world.

Finding Our Joy

Stop waiting to be happy! It's right in front of you. You can have joy; you just need to reach out and grab it. These are real words to live by. We all go through life with moments that may not feel the best. Maybe it's the emotional stress from a relationship, work, or being a parent. No one said it was going to be comfortable navigating through life's countless barrage of stressors.

There are a million obstacles that distract us daily. Sometimes we get upset, angry, and sad. Sadly, if we continue these patterns, it can be easy to forget what it's like to have joy.

I've fallen prey to this pattern many times. Having thoughts that the world had crashed down on me and I was being dealt a *"crappy hand,"* I slowly let joy slip away. As I went through my last divorce, I clearly remember thinking how unfair life was and that I wasn't worthy of having happiness.

It was then that I started allowing my daily routines of self-loathing to create a trend. It's not something I'm proud of looking back on and indeed not a place I want to go again.

When you comprehend and rationalize the thought that you deserve to be happy, a better life opens up, and opportunities arise. Your faults and doubts will get swept up and blown out to sea. At this point, there's nothing that can slow us down when we see ourselves deserving of joy and peace. Our fears will no longer have hold of us.

If you think you aren't willing to make changes, you're going to have to ask yourself the hard questions. What is it I want? What do I expect to happen if I do nothing? Am I afraid of getting disappointed or failing?

If you want to blossom into your true potential, you can't be afraid of changes. We often neglect ourselves first because we don't view ourselves as someone worthy of love. It could be that this message is something that we've heard over and over again in life, relationships, and career. Maybe it's a perception we're used to hearing. Either way, why should we continue to perpetuate the myth? If there are things we can do to help us reach *Joy* and *Love*, then we must try.

I can't give you any magical outcomes. I can't tell you the easy road towards joy and happiness. The real question becomes: can we chase what we know is right, even if we know that it won't erase all the pain**?**

It's tough to chase something that you don't know the outcome of. We have to have faith; the result will be that of joy and acceptance.

Facing Our Fears

Fear and anxiety can last for a short stint and then eventually pass, or it can last longer, possibly taking over your life. I've had fear take over my love for life. It affected my ability to eat, sleep, concentrate, even leave the house and go to work. It can hold you back from what you want and also affect your health.

It can be easy to become overwhelmed by your fears. Fear of rejection, loneliness, not being worthy of love: these feelings will eat you alive if you let them.

After my first divorce, everything unravelled many times more than I had expected. I lost my kids to the fears I was holding close to me. I wanted to be the best father I could, but fear kept me back. I didn't want to disappoint. I felt like a failure not holding the marriage together. I can tell you firsthand, looking back, this attitude got me nowhere. The actions I took were informed by my fears, and the actions I wanted to take were held back by them. I wish I had done things differently.

Going through two divorces and family issues was devastating. It seemed unfathomable at the time. I had to believe that I was doing what was right for me and that I would someday have joy in my life. Facing your fears does not always bring instant results. It could be days, months, and years before you are free of them. But I can look back now with no doubts or regret for where I've been or where I'll go.

Listen, fears aren't all bad; at times, they can be useful. They challenge us and make us stronger. We've all encountered fears that have challenged us to overcome what we previously thought impossible.

Believe it or not, writing this book was a huge fear of mine. I wouldn't have considered doing it if my wife had not encouraged me to do so. It was really out of my comfort zone. Writing didn't come first nature to me. I'm sure it was the fear of the unknown. What would people think? Would I be rejected, disappointed, or humiliated? These were all the things running through my mind.

I finally got up the courage to give it a go, and I haven't looked back since. I realize now that the best things in life can come from facing your fears. It may not always work out. Maybe you'll fall flat on our face. The one thing I do know is that you won't know the outcome if you don't try.

Final Thoughts

Small moments. They're something we all have: things in our lives that tend to get passed up or unnoticed, most likely underappreciated. We take them for granted because we're so used to having them, or they happen so often it's as if they're a part of our daily routine.

We've become a society filled with grand celebrations. Birthdays, graduations, and job promotions are incredible milestones and, as such, should be celebrated. But what about those daily rituals, like getting your child ready for school, cooking dinner for the family, or chatting with friends. Maybe if we made it a habit of embracing those things, we would start to understand how amazing our lives are. Beautiful things are happening all around us, and it's those little moments that can bring you the inner peace you desire.

Don't let fear be the deciding factor in your life. Fear can hold you down and destroy your hopes and dreams. If we let fear dictate how we choose to live, over time it has the ability to grow roots and put down permanent scars. When this happens, anxiousness, loneliness, and doubt slowly creep in. The years of pure joy and happiness always play second fiddle, taking away our right to the pleasure we all deserve. I've had fears run my life for years, and over time fear put self-doubt and loss of trust at the forefront.

We're all going to experience fears at some point in our lives, whether they're personal or come from the external environments around us. As a society, we are bombarded by the news and the internet daily. It can be overwhelming at times.

I get it. Today more than ever, we've had to deal with tragedies far and near. The world has had to deal with hurricanes, earthquakes, and the recent COVID-19 pandemic. These are sensitive times for all, and it can be hard to see the light at the end of the tunnel.

The positive side is that there is a crucial and rewarding connection between our thoughts, both personal and global. Forgiving ourselves, finding our joy, and facing our fears can have a profound effect on our health and on our connection with one another. We, as a society, can harness and destroy the damaging effect of the tragedies by learning how to respond to our fears.

I've included a forgiveness guide to help you identify some fears and joys in your own life. Head over to healthmindsoul.com and download your copy.

It's ok to debate your fears. Just remember it's a debate you should always win

~ JS

Forgiveness: Fears and Joy

Today I choose to embrace my true self

1. List 3 people you're willing to forgive

Ex: a friend, family, co-worker

A. _____

B. _____

C. _____

2. List 3 things that bring you joy

Ex: family, career, health, friends

A. _____

B. _____

C. _____

3. What fears do you struggle with?

_____

_____

4. What emotional armour do you wear? How can you work on removing it?

_____

_____

FINDING YOUR INSPIRATION

So here we are! You've waded through all this material, filling yourself full of possibilities and dreams. I hope that all this information will further your knowledge and expand your potential when it comes to opening the door to your new life. Even if it's just to explore new ideas, it's your chance to make the changes necessary to see results.

I can say with confidence now that if you had asked me three or four years ago if I would be at this point in my life, I would have said that's crazy talk. If you had told me that I would venture out to things like meditation, spirituality and the Law of Attraction, I'm sure I would have told you that's not me. I walked around with a closed mind and a guarded heart.

I've been lucky enough to have found my way. Unfortunately, it took several marriages and heartache to get there. But it also included maturation and growth. I'm incredibly grateful for the opportunity that presented itself to me, and lucky enough to have an amazingly beautiful and smart wife introduce me to this lifestyle of health, mind and soul. Since then I've been on the ride of a lifetime.

This is your chance to help yourself. It's time to add a few more lessons into your already kick-ass life. Even if you take just one thing away from this book, your life is going to change for the better.

I wanted to finish this last chapter on a high; really throw out all the stops and get you excited for what's to come. It's time to unleash those positive vibrations out into the universe.

Dream Big

As I alluded to early on, I was that Dream Medium guy. Yes, I was full of dreams, but they were very calculated and extremely safe. I never tried to *"reach for the stars."* In my mind it meant when things didn't go as planned, I wouldn't have that far to fall. I wanted to be close to the ground, safe from the fall, safe from scrutiny. I constantly doubted myself and feared that what I had to offer wasn't good enough.

Don't let that be the case for you. If someone comes asking you if you have something to offer, you damn well better tell them the answer is *YES*. We all have something to offer. You might not know what it is, but don't worry. The universe will let you know exactly what it is.

I sit here now, writing a book that I love and am proud to have written. I wrote over 90% of it on my phone. Yes, that's right. I could have easily awoken from my sleep and said, *"It's just a dream, it was a cool idea, but no thanks,"* but I didn't. My wife told me I should do it and she had my back from start to finish. This was my time and my dream and I was going to see it through. Nothing was going to stop me.

Don't let anything stop you. If you want it bad enough, you'll find ways to make it happen, regardless of the obstacles that might stand in your way. I've worked extremely hard to give you all the tools you need to set a path that is right for you. Only you know what that path is, and it's your job to make it the best one possible. From epiphany to reality, I always say. You never know what will present itself. You just need to be ready and open to what comes your way.

Never Give Up

We all have our moments where we've been down and out. But it's your choice to come headstrong at it and turn it around. I'm not the first person to persevere through life, and I won't be the last.

We all have day-to-day struggles and some that just seem insurmountable. I can tell you that no matter what it feels like at the moment, there will be a point in time when life is right again. I hope the information throughout this book will help you in your endeavours. Remember, you're on this journey for a short time. If you want your life to be as positive and happy as possible, it doesn't matter what your current situation is. Make it *"your best."*

Follow Your Heart

I believe you must follow your heart if you want to succeed in life. Life is short, and you shouldn't waste your time doing things that your heart, mind, and soul genuinely don't desire. This can be applied to most situations: careers, relationships, and life aspirations in general.

Most people just do what they're told and try to get by, but that isn't how we should be. We all deserve to be happy and live our fullest lives possible. We know our mind and heart are going to be fighting back and forth with each other if we're in a situation that we are not 100% sure about.

I jumped into a relationship with someone too soon after my first marriage. My mind and heart were always in constant debate. Why? Because my head was going to try to talk me into all the reasons why I should stay. My heart was still going to fight for what I wanted.

I can tell you, if you aren't satisfied with your life then you will spend your days in a constant battle. But when you make that change, remember it's going to be tough. There's the adage that the grass isn't always greener on the other side for a reason. Because if you are anything like me, then you hate giving up and letting your friends and family down. But I can tell you that your friends and family would rather you be invested in something that you can give your all to than in something you aren't sold on.

You should always follow your heart. It will take you to heights you never thought possible. Your spirit still wants to pursue your dreams and make you happier than anything possible. It's your centre of love and happiness.

Put Out to the Universe What You Want Back!

It's hard to believe how far I've come over the years, especially when it relates to the Law of Attraction. I went from a nonexistence of beliefs to beliefs that have far exceeded my expectations.

What happens to the energy you put out into the universe? The universe throws it right back at you. Everything you project out into the universe will be sent right back at you. This is a more unique way of saying treat people how you want to be treated. Your feelings, thoughts, words, and actions are sources of energy. You are in complete control of that energy. What you give to the universe it will give back to you plus more than what you imagined you would get out of life. It is so important to understand this aspect of reality. It takes years to master this, but nothing great ever comes easy.

Go out today and give the people what you want to be given. Give the universe what you want to be given. The universe repays in bigger rewards. Follow your heart and don't let thoughts cloud your judgment.

Try to keep the positive thoughts flowing, keep the energy high, and only allow the vibrations of those positive people around you to influence how you feel. When you're in a high state of being, it's incredible how you start to attract the energy of the positive people around you. Positive situations begin to present themselves, and the negative people and conditions begin to dissipate. It's because of the higher frequency that you're able to shape your life the way you choose.

The Law of Attraction states that what you put out to the universe is what you'll receive. Give positive, and you'll receive positive. Project negativity, and it will also be returned. I believe that while we may not have control of every situation that happens to us, we are in control of how we respond to the situation. This, to me, is the most important factor. It defines who we are and what we want to be.

Don't Let Age Define You

I've heard time and again how you're too young to dream or you're over the hill. But you can never be too young or too old to start following your dreams! It's time to start dreaming now; what better way than today to begin your journey. Don't wait for it to come to you. Let that someday be today. Start living your life and showing the world what you have to offer.

Age should have no consideration on how much you can achieve. Any idea can spark another approach that can be a springboard for the rest of your life.

Many companies have been created by those under the age of 18. They followed their desires and branded their own businesses. Same goes for those individuals that have lived a full life and then started another career or two.

I can certainly attest to that. At the age of 44, I've worked 20 years of my life as a Biomedical Technologist fixing medical equipment in hospitals. I can say with absolute certainty that it's brought me much joy and happiness. Having said that, I have now turned a passion for writing into a book. Don't be afraid to step outside your comfort zone and try something new. Maybe it's a new hobby or career. Whatever you decide, believe in it. Keep dreaming and follow your passion.

Pay It Forward

Why is being generous such a mood-booster? One reason is that it gives you a strong sense you're doing something that matters. There are a lot of positive social consequences to being kind. People appreciate you, they're grateful, and they might reciprocate.

Have you ever had someone provide something of value that you found related to your life and had special meaning? They didn't do it because they had to, but because they wanted to.

I never forget the time, money, or effort someone spends on me, with or without knowing. We live in a fast-moving world, and it's easy to forget the kindness that surrounds us.

Paying it forward makes the person doing it feel great. If you're one of those people, things are fantastic! Paying it forward also makes the person being helped feel unique and essential. If you're on the receiving end, things are also excellent!

Next time you're out, pay for someone's goods unexpectedly. Every time we raise the vibrations of others, we raise the awareness in others to do well.

Don't Let Technology Dictate Your Life

It wasn't too many years ago that I was using the internet as an escape from the day-to-day hustle of everyday life. The same does not hold now, and it couldn't be more the opposite as I now connect with the real world to escape the onslaught of technology.

I'm very aware of the beneficial uses of technology. I love it and use all aspects of it daily. I just don't want it to control my life. It's impressive to access anything at our fingertips, but can we go 10 minutes without looking at our phones or computers?

I think it's more important than ever to take time out. Most of us have heard the buzz phrase *"digital detox."* It's a great way to take a deep breath and enjoy some time without the distraction of technology and social media. I can tell you that one day away from your phone might seem like an eternity, but life will still go on with or without your *"likes."*

Take even a few hours each week to silence your phone and reconnect with something else you're passionate about. Enjoy 30 minutes reading, writing or journaling. Go for a walk or meditate. Getting in tune with yourself and nature is amazing therapy for the soul.

As we all know, technology is eliminating our up-close communication with others. We use our phones thousands of times a day. It's no wonder we've lost our communication skills. We were once a society that paused to chat or say hello to others as we passed them in the hallways of work, school, or the mall. Nowadays, we walk around mindless with our heads bent over glued to a text or social media feed without a glimpse of the world going on around us.

Next time you think of wishing someone a happy birthday or sending congratulations, try using the phone feature on your cell or telling them face-to-face. Nothing will cheer someone up more than that.

You Must Learn to Love Yourself

Learning to love yourself and truly make it a priority is one of the most challenging things to do. We must learn to take time out of our busy lives and put ourselves as the priority, focusing on your own needs. I realize this can be extremely hard as we're surrounded by colleagues, friends, and family the majority of the day – which leaves little time for *YOU*.

I understand this can be difficult at first, as we're programmed to put others first. Spouses, children, loved ones all command attention and time from us. The realization will soon set in that before you can take care of others you must take care of yourself. It's completely ok to have your own time. It might feel a little selfish at first, but with the right tools and time management anything is possible.

I set aside 10 minutes in the morning before going to work to meditate and journal. After work, it's straight to the gym. Before bed, I make sure I get in at least 30 minutes of writing or reading. Don't be afraid to set aside time for you.

Attitude of Gratitude

I've always felt that if you want to be sure you wake up every day on the right side of the bed and with a positive mindset, you're going to need to have an attitude of gratitude. You have to make it a priority to appreciate everything about your amazing life.

I realize we're going to have days, maybe even weeks, where things aren't going the way we want. We will, however, need to remember to keep a grateful mindset and loving heart so that when moments of hardship or despair strike, we don't lose our true essence.

Final Thoughts

If you've ever wanted to start a project, career, or business, first off I want to say do it! Absolutely do it! Yes, it can be tiresome, drawn-out, and scary, but also downright exciting at the same time. Find something you're passionate about and give it a go. Don't let anything hold you back from achieving your goals and dreams. Just know that, like most things in life, when you're venturing out on your own, having the support of friends, family, and loved ones on your side is invaluable.

It took me a long time to finally buy into the fact that something can and will happen if you want it badly enough. I wasn't sure if this book would succeed or fail in the eyes of others, but what I do know is that I poured my heart and soul into it. That effort alone will always make it a success to me. Don't stop chasing your dreams, and don't ever doubt that you're not good enough. There's more than enough greatness to go around.

I hope that you enjoyed the challenges and worksheets throughout the book. Maybe they inspired and pushed you to examine and pursue new ventures. It's through repetition and perseverance you start to make headway on what seems to be a substantial upward battle. Keep at it and continue to work hard. Start your new workout routines, begin your nutrition plan, continue working on your relationships, and journal daily. As you incorporate each section into your new life, it won't be long before it seems like second nature. It won't be long before you feel like you've been doing it for years.

I want to thank you from the bottom of my heart for following me on this journey. Many months of writing are coming to an end. I hope that you enjoyed your time and were able to take things away that might light a passion in you.

~ Jeff Simpson

TARA'S STORY: HER LIFE, HER VISION

My wife and co-author on this book has been instrumental in my life and opened my eyes to the kindness and abundance the universe has in store for us. I wanted her to share some stories and answer some questions from her point of view as she has so much to give. Her perspective comes across in careers, relationships, journaling, reading, and healthy living. She has taught me so much in each area. I hope you take away as much as I did.

How has your career journey led to joy and fulfillment?

In the beginning, my career brought me joy in ways of travel experiences, meeting new friends, and shopping for clothes on the weekends. When I found a job that I loved, my happiness came from many more important things like working hard for goals that had a positive impact on my family and helping others achieve financial or health success.

I found fulfillment in working hard, educating myself at what I did, and investing time and money to grow, so I could be my best self for my family, clients, business partners, and friends. I felt a sense of pride in teaching and training others to be successful while also having more time for their families.

How have your relationships shaped the person you are today?

I have learned so much from past and current relationships. You learn from previous relationships what you don't want to bring into existing ones. And there are some things you discover that you keep and bring those great lessons with you to your current and new relationships.

The great relationships I've had have shaped me to be a more positive, spiritual, and giving person. I've had a few great teachers along the way, and I'm so grateful for their foresight and wisdom. I incorporate their lessons into my current and new relationships. These intuitive nuggets have given me the chance to have authentic, real, and heart-centred connections with beautiful people.

When did you start to immerse yourself in journaling and reading?

I was never one to read or journal. After starting my online health & wellness business, it was suggested by a successful colleague that I should start to read books related to our profession and also papers relating to personal growth, and to start journaling.

I thought I was *"good"* and didn't need those tools. Oh, was I wrong! If someone is more successful and they tell you to read personal growth books and start a gratitude journal, you do it! I wanted to be successful like them, so I was going to take their advice and run with it.

After immersing myself in personal growth, self-development books, and journaling daily, things started to shift. I began to attract the things I've wanted to see happen. More positive outcomes began coming my way. Things started to happen more easily and quickly. My mindset was forever happy and positive.

What are the biggest takeaways and recommendations you have for others?

- Write down your goals – including personal, business, career, life, health, relationship, and financial
- Have a dream board
- Surround yourself with positive, kind, and giving people
- Reduce the time with negative people
- Read personal growth books all the time
- Journal – including gratitude, goals, dreams, and positive affirmations
- Live your life on purpose, help others, give to others when possible
- Teach your children the value of being kind to others. Teach them to read personal growth books and to journal their gratitude
- Dream Big!
- Treat your body like a temple and take care of it on the inside & out – work out & eat healthily
- Get good quality sleep
- Say *"I love you"* more than necessary
- Praise others when they do a great job
- Make people feel special
- Say Thank You

What is your definition of living a healthy lifestyle?

My definition of living a healthy lifestyle may be different from others. I consider it a holistic living: Mind & Body approach from the inside & out. I believe it's essential to move your body daily at a sport or activity you love, including something that's challenging to your physical body with weight resistance and cardio. I feel it's essential to fuel your body with nutrient-dense foods, incorporating plant-based and balanced meal plans.

Self-care is so important as well. Find out what makes you relaxed, happy, or feel Zen-like, and do it often. Is it eating healthy foods or exercising regularly? Whatever it is you do, make sure you move your body, get great quality sleep, laugh out loud and, most of all, have some *"YOU"* time. These are all things we can do to help.

What drives you to have so much passion for your healthy lifestyle?

I want to be happy and healthy for the rest of my life! We can do many positive things to help our bodies function at their full and most vigorous capacity. If we can help just one person live their most optimal life, we can start to make little changes in a big world.

ACKNOWLEDGEMENT

It's been an amazing rollercoaster of a journey over the last several months writing this book. It's had so many ups and downs. I've opened myself up to the world and professed my vulnerability, which was extremely hard at times. I know now I'm better off for it.

I wanted to make sure I acknowledged those that helped me through the process. I couldn't have done this without my co-author and partner in crime, Tara. My wife is amazing from top to bottom and encouraged me from day one. Yes, literally from day one. She told me how there wasn't anything holding me back from writing this book and achieving my dreams. It certainly wasn't the path I was thinking about, but through the grace of the universe, I am where I am today. Thank you for being there for me.

THESE BOOKS WILL CHANGE YOUR LIFE!

Life
You Are a Badass ~ Jen Sincero

Career
The 10X Rule ~ Grant Cardone

Relationships
The 5 Love Languages ~ Gary Chapman

Law of Attraction
The Secret ~ Rhonda Byrne

Meditation
Super Attractor ~Gabrielle Bernstein

Gratitude and Fears
Daring Greatly ~ Brené Brown
The School of Greatness ~ Lewis Howes

REFERENCES

Ref 1
- URL: https://www.zdnet.com/article/americans-spend-far-more-time-on-their-smartphones-than-they-think/
- Website Title: ZDNet
- Publication Day: 28
- Publication Month: April
- Publication Year: 2019
- Article Title: Americans spend far more time on their smartphones than they think

Ref 2
- URL: https://www.sciencenewsforstudents.org/article/new-health-risk-too-much-screentime-sitting
- Website Title: Science News for Students
- Publication Day: 06
- Publication Month: December
- Publication Year: 2019
- Article Title: New risk from too much screentime

Ref 3
- URL: https://onlinelibrary.wiley.com/doi/abs/10.1111/j.2044-8295.1997.tb02622.x
- Website Title: Wiley Online Library
- Publication Day:13
- Publication Month: April
- Publication Year: 2011
- Article Title: The psychological impact of negative TV news bulletins: The catastrophizing of personal worries

Ref 4
- URL: https://www.researchgate.net/publication/14149927_The_psychological_impact_of_negative_TV_news_bulletins_The_catastrophizing_of_personal_worries
- Website Title: ResearchGate
- Publication Day: 07
- Publication Month: October
- Publication Year: 2020
- Article Title: (PDF) The psychological impact of negative TV news bulletins: The catastrophizing of personal worries

Ref 5
- URL: https://sites.psu.edu/siowfa16/2016/09/13/the-effects-texting-has-on-communication/
- Website Title: SiOWfa:16 Science in Our World: Certainty and Controversy
- Publication Day: 13
- Publication Month: September
- Publication Year: 2016
- Access Day: 12
- Access Month: May
- Access Year: 2020
- Article Title: The Effects Texting has on Communication

Ref 6
- URL: https://www.health.harvard.edu/ staying-healthy/blue-light-has-a-dark-side
- Website Title: Harvard Health
- Article Title: Blue light has a dark side
- Publication Year: 2012

Ref 7
- URL: https://www.healthline.com/health/ fast-food-effects-on-body
- Website Title: Healthline
- Article Title: The Effects of Fast Food on the Body - healthline.com
- Publication Year: 2018

Ref 8
- URL: https://www.businessinsider.com/ disturbing-facts-about-your-job-2011-2
- Website Title: Business Insider
- Publication Day: 02
- Publication Month: August
- Publication Year: 2018
- Article Title:17 seriously disturbing facts about your job

Ref 9
- URL: http://www.chiswickconsulting.com/ho w-important-is-self-esteem-in-the-workplace/
- Website Title: Chiswick Consulting
- Publication Day: 06
- Publication Month: July
- Publication Year: 2015
- Article Title: How important is self-esteem in the workplace?

Ref 10
- URL: https://thriveglobal.com/stories/impact-of-healthy-wor k-environment-on-your-performance/
- Website Title: Thrive Global
- Article Title: Impact of Healthy Work Environment on Your Performance
- Publication Year: 2019

Ref 11
- URL: https://www.healthyworksofpa.com/benefits-of-a-healthy-work-environment/
- Website Title: HealthyWorks
- Publication Day: 03
- Publication Month: October
- Publication Year: 2016
- Article Title: Benefits of a Healthy Work Environment

Ref 12
- URL: https://www.healthline.com/nutrition/12-benefits-of-meditation#TOC_TITLE_HDR_2
- Website Title: Healthline
- Article Title: 12 Science-Based Benefits of Meditation

Ref 13
- URL: http://www.simplifyinginterfaces.com/2008/08/01/95-percent-of-brain-activity-is-beyo nd-our-conscious-awareness/
- Website Title: Neurosciences UX
- Publication Day: 01
- Publication Month: August
- Publication Year: 2008
- Article Title: 95 percent of brain activity is beyond our conscious awareness

Ref 14

- URL: https://vickitidwellpalmer.com/ refocus-your-view-with-gratitud e-the-6-skill-for-building-intimacy/
- Website Title: Vicki Tidwell Palmer
- Publication Day: 30
- Publication Month: December
- Publication Year: 2019
- Article Title: Refocus Your View With Gratitude: The #6 Skill for Building Intimacy

Ref 15

- URL: https://www.health.harvard.edu/ healthbeat/ giving-thanks-can-make-you-happier
- Website Title: Harvard Health Publishing
- Publication Day: 28
- Publication Month: March
- Publication Year: 2019
- Article Title: Giving thanks can make you happier

Ref 16

- URL: https://oconnellfuneralhomes.com/ affirmation-thanks/
- Website Title: O' Connell's Family Funeral Home
- Article Title: Thank You

Ref 17

- URL: https://eocinstitute.org/meditation/ dhea_gaba_cortisol_hgh_melatonin_ serotonin_endorphins/
- Website Title: EOC Institute
- Article Title: How Meditation Boosts Melatonin, Serotonin, GABA, DHEA, Endorphins, Growth Hormone, & More

Ref 18
- URL: https://www.cnbc.com/2019/01/29/24-percent-of-american-adults-havent-read-a-book-in-the-past-year--heres-why-.html
- Website Title: CNBC
- Publication Day: 29
- Publication Month: January
- Publication Year: 2019
- Access Day: 12
- Access Month: May
- Access Year: 2020
- Article Title: 24 percent of American adults haven't read a book in the past year – here's why

Ref 19
- URL: https://www.lifehack.org/articles/lifestyle/10-benefits-reading-why-you-should-read-everyday.html
- Website Title: Lifehack
- Publication Day: 17
- Publication Month: March
- Publication Year: 2020
- Access Day: 12
- Access Month: May
- Access Year: 2020
- Article Title: 10 Benefits of Reading: Why You Should Read Every Day

Ref 20
- URL: https://www.telegraph.co.uk/news/health/news/5070874/Reading-can-help-reduce-stress.html
- Website Title: The Telegraph
- Publication Day: 30
- Publication Month: March
- Publication Year: 2009
- Article Title: Reading 'can help reduce stress'

Ref 21
- URL: https://medium.com/the-mission/how-to-use-the-reading-habits-of-billionaires-to-radically-improve-your-intelligence-and-success-9c24647e2b59
- Website Title: Medium
- Publication Day: 21
- Publication Month: November
- Publication Year: 2016
- Article Title: How To Use The Reading Habits of Billionaires To Radically Improve Your Intelligence and Success

Ref 22
- URL: https://www.bustle.com/p/why-reading-is-the-best-workout-for-your-brain-57441
- Website Title: Bustle
- Publication Day: 15
- Publication Month: May
- Publication Year: 2017
- Article Title: How Reading Improves Your Memory

Ref 23
- URL: https://intermountainhealthcare.org/blogs/topics/live-well/2018/07/5-powerful-health-benefits-of-journaling/
- Website Title: intermountainhealthcare.org
- Article Title: 5 Powerful Health Benefits of Journaling

Ref 24
- URL: https://exploringyourmind.com/trust-generosity-affection-the-benefits-of-oxytocin/
- Website Title: Exploring your mind
- Publication Month: May
- Publication Year: 2020

- Article Title: Oxytocin: the interesting effects of the love hormone

Ref 25
- Book Title: *The 5 Love Languages*
- Book Publisher: Northfield Pub.
- Publication Year: 2015

Ref 26
- URL: http://cyberdoktor.org/en/2-cyberdoktor-org/179-the-new-science-we-are-made-of-energy-not-matter
- Website Title: cyberdoktor.org
- Article Title: The new Science: We are made of Energy, not Matter

Ref 27
- URL: https://www.wanderlustworker.com/3-ways-to-manifest-money-using-the-law-of-attraction/
- Website Title: Wanderlust Worker
- Publication Day: 02
- Publication Month: December
- Publication Year: 2019
- Article Title: 3 Ways To Manifest Money Using The Law Of Attraction

Ref 28
- URL: https://arthritisashley.com/2014/02/24/the-law-of-attraction-and-chronic-illness-by-ashley-boynes-shuck/
- Website Title: arthritisashley.com
- Publication Day: 24
- Publication Month: February
- Publication Year: 2014
- Article Title: The Law of Attraction and Chronic Illness – by Ashley Boynes-Shuck

Ref 29
- URL: https://anotherlevelhealth.com/
- Website Title: Another Level Health
- Article Title: Another Level Health

Ref 30
- URL: https://medlineplus.gov/benefitsof exercise.html
- Website Title: MedlinePlus
- Publication Day: 04
- Publication Month: October
- Publication Year: 2019
- Article Title: Benefits of Exercise

Ref 31
- URL: https://www.wfc.org/website/index. php?option=com_content&view=article&id =90&lang=en
- Website Title: World Federation of Chiropractic
- Article Title: Definition of Chiropractic

Ref 32
- URL: https://well.blogs.nytimes. com/2015/10/05/chiropractic-care-grows-an d-gains-acceptance/
- Website Title: The New York Times
- Publication Day: 05
- Publication Month: October
- Publication Year: 2015
- Article Title: Chiropractic Care Grows, and Gains Acceptance

Ref 33
- URL: https://www.mayoclinic.org/tests-procedures/massage-therapy/about/ pac-20384595
- Website Title: Mayo Clinic
- Publication Day: 07

- Publication Month: November
- Publication Year: 2018
- Article Title: Massage therapy

Ref 34
- URL: https://www.mayoclinic.org/ healthy-lifestyle/fitness/in-depth/exercise/ art-20045517
- Website Title: Mayo Clinic
- Publication Day: 09
- Publication Month: July
- Publication Year: 2019
- Article Title: Aerobic exercise: How to warm up and cool down

Ref 35
- URL: https://www.medicalnewstoday.com/ articles/325353
- Website Title: Medical News Today
- Publication Day: 31
- Publication Month: May
- Publication Year: 2019
- Article Title: Why sleep is essential for health

Ref 36
- URL: https://www.health. harvard.edu/healthbeat/ giving-thanks-can-make-you-happier
- Website Title: Harvard Health Publishing
- Article Title: Giving thanks can make you happier

Ref 37
- URL: https://www.happyfeed.co/research/ what-is-a-gratitude-journal
- Website Title: Happyfeed
- Article Title: What is a Gratitude Journal?

Ref 38
- URL: https://mindbliss.com/ gratitude-meditation/
- Website Title: Mindbliss
- Publication Day: 14
- Publication Month: February
- Publication Year: 2019
- Article Title: Gratitude Meditation: Mastering the Art of Being Intentionally Thankful

Ref 39
- URL: https://www.readersdigest. co.uk/health/health-conditions/ the-healing-power-of-gratitude
- Website Title: Reader's Digest
- Publication Day: 01
- Publication Month: January
- Publication Year: 2017
- Article Title: The healing power of gratitude

Ref 40
- URL: https://www.psychologytoday.com/ca/ blog/what-mentally-strong-people-dont- do/201504/7-scientifically -proven-benefits-gratitude
- Website Title: Psychology Today
- Publication Day: 03
- Publication Month: April
- Publication Year: 2015
- Article Title: 7 Scientifically Proven Benefits of Gratitude

Ref 41
- URL: https://www.psychologytoday.com/ ca/blog/two-takes-depression/201211/ how-gratitude-combats-depression
- Website Title: Psychology Today
- Publication Day: 26

- Publication Month: November
- Publication Year: 2012
- Article Title: How Gratitude Combats Depression

Ref 42
- URL: https://www.psychologytoday.com/ca/blog/what-mentally-strong-people-dont-do/201504/7-scientifically-proven-benefits-gratitude
- Website Title: Psychology Today
- Publication Day: 03
- Publication Month: April
- Publication Year: 2015
- Article Title: 7 Scientifically Proven Benefits of Gratitude

Ref 43
- URL: https://www.spine-health.com/conditions/neck-pain/how-does-text-neck-cause-pain
- Website Title: Spine
- Access Day: 12
- Access Month: May
- Access Year: 2020
- Article Title: How Does Text Neck Cause Pain?

Ref 44
- URL: http://www.antilogyyoga.com/yoga.html#sthash.5fv9HCuv.dpbs
- Website Title: Antilogy Yoga
- Access Day: 12
- Access Month: May
- Access Year: 2020
- Article Title: Yoga

Ref 45
Mike Conners, BScPT, FCAMPT, Physiotherapist

Ref 46
- URL: https://en.wikipedia.org/meditation
- Website Title: Wikipedia
- Publication Day: 02
- Publication Month: October
- Publication Year: 2020
- Article Title: Meditation

Ref 47
- URL: https://www.jackcanfield.com/blog/ utilizing-the-law-of-attraction/
- Website Title: Jack Canfield
- Publication Day: 02
- Publication Month: December
- Publication Year: 2019
- Access Day: 17
- Access Month: August
- Access Year: 2020
- Article Title: Utilizing The Law of Attraction

Ref 48
- URL: https://www.defensivedriving.com/blog/ distracted-driving-statistics/
- Website Title: DefensiveDriving.com
- Access Day: 20
- Access Month: August
- Access Year: 2020
- Article Title: Distracted Driving Statistics

Ref 49
Jan Gonda (1963), The Indian Mantra, Oriens, Vol. 16, pages 244–297

Ref 50
- Book Title: *The Mask of Masculinity: How Men Can Embrace Vulnerability, Create Strong Relationships, and Live Their Fullest Lives*
- Book Publisher: Rodale Books
- Publication Year: 2017

HEALTH
MIND
SOUL

Authors : Jeff Simpson ~ Tara Clements
@healthmindsoullife | www.healthmindsoul.com
Health Mind Soul Lifestyle & Wellness

Jeff Simpson was born and raised in California. After spending ten years as a Hospital Corpsman in the U.S. Navy, he ventured into his current career as a Biomedical Technologist. He currently works at the IWK Health Centre in Halifax, NS. Jeff has ventured from the West to East Coast and now has his roots firmly planted in Nova Scotia, Canada, where he lives with his wife and family. His passion for a healthy lifestyle has driven him to inspire people to live their most optimal life. Jeff is producing his own brand Health Mind Soul Lifestyle & Wellness in the hopes of helping others find balance.

CPSIA information can be obtained
at www.ICGtesting.com
Printed in the USA
BVHW031527291120
594144BV00003B/18